THE PEOPLE'S REPUBLIC OF CHINA (PRC) continues to pursue a long-term, comprehensive military modernization program designed to improve the capacity of its armed forces to fight and win short-duration, high-intensity regional contingencies. Preparing for potential conflict in the Taiwan Strait, which includes deterring or defeating third-party intervention, remains the focus and primary driver of China's military investment. However, the Chinese People's Liberation Army (PLA) also is placing emphasis on preparing for contingencies other than Taiwan, including potential contingencies in the South and East China Seas. The October 2013 MANEUVER-5 exercise in the Philippine Sea, which included participation from all three PLA navy fleets – the North Sea Fleet, the East Sea Fleet, and the South Sea Fleet – was the largest PLA Navy open-ocean exercise seen to date. Additionally, China conducted the three-part MISSION ACTION series of joint military exercises over a six week period during September and October. These exercises combined PLA ground, navy and air forces in large-scale maneuvers along China's southern and southeastern coasts. As China's interests, capabilities, and international influence have grown, its military modernization program has also become increasingly focused on military investments for a range of missions beyond China's coast, including sea lane security, counterpiracy, peacekeeping, and humanitarian assistance/disaster relief (HA/DR).

China's leaders describe modernization of the PLA as essential to preserving and sustaining what they view as a "period of strategic opportunity" to advance China's national development during the first two decades of the 21st century. China's leaders see this period as providing an opportunity to focus on fostering a stable external environment to provide the PRC the strategic space to prioritize economic growth and development and to achieve "national rejuvenation" by 2049. At the same time, Chinese leaders express a desire to maintain peace and stability along their country's periphery; expand their diplomatic influence to facilitate access to markets, capital, and resources; and avoid direct confrontation with the United States and other countries. This strategy has led to a growing Chinese presence in regions all over the world, and particularly on its periphery, creating new and expanding economic and diplomatic interests. China's expanding interests have led to friction between some of its regional neighbors, including allies and partners of the United States.

i

Although the dialogue between the United States and China is improving, outstanding questions remain about the rate of growth in China's military expenditures due to the lack of transparency regarding China's intentions. In 2013, China announced a 5.7 percent increase in its annual military budget to $119.5 billion, continuing more than two decades of sustained annual defense spending increases. China sustained its investments in strategic forces modernization, as well as key anti-access/area-denial (A2/AD) capabilities such as advanced intermediate- and medium-range conventional ballistic missiles, long-range land-attack and anti-ship cruise missiles, counter-space weapons, and offensive cyber capabilities. China's military investments provide it with a growing ability to project power at increasingly longer ranges. In 2013, this included at-sea testing of China's first aircraft carrier and continued development of fifth generation fighter aircraft.

During his visit to California in June 2013 for a summit with President Obama, China's President Xi Jinping and President Obama affirmed that China and the United States should continue working together to build a "new model" of relations in order to expand practical areas of cooperation and constructively manage differences in the bilateral relationship. During a robust number of high-level U.S.-China political and military engagements in 2013, leaders from both countries agreed that "enhanced and substantive" military dialogue and communication would foster greater understanding and expand mutual trust. Within that framework, the U.S. Department of Defense seeks to continue building a military-to-military relationship with China that is sustained and substantive, while encouraging China to contribute constructively to efforts with the United States, our allies and partners, and the greater international community to maintain peace and stability. As the United States builds a stronger foundation for a military-to-military relationship with China, it also will continue to monitor China's evolving military strategy, doctrine, and force development and encourage China to be more transparent about its military modernization program. In concert with its allies and partners, the United States will continue adapting its forces, posture, and operational concepts to maintain a stable and secure Asia-Pacific security environment.

1

ANNUAL UPDATE

This chapter provides a brief synopsis of significant developments in Chinese military and security activities over the course of the past year, with an emphasis on those activities specifically highlighted in section 1246 of the National Defense Authorization Act for Fiscal Year 2010 (P.L. 111-84).

DEVELOPMENTS IN CHINA'S BILATERAL OR MULTILATERAL RELATIONSHIPS

China's military engagement with other countries seeks to enhance China's international presence and influence by improving relationships with foreign militaries, bolstering China's international and regional image, and assuaging other countries' concerns about China's rise. The PLA's engagement activities assist its modernization through the acquisition of advanced weapon systems and technologies, increased operational experience, and access to foreign military practices, doctrine, and training methods.

In December 2013, the *PLA Daily*, the official newspaper of the Chinese military, published its top ten highlights of China's military diplomacy in 2013. This list focused on military exercises and overseas deployments, including the China-Russia naval exercise in July 2013, the China-U.S. disaster management exercise held in November 2013, the deployment of troops for the UN Multidimensional Integrated Stabilization Mission in Mali (MINUSMA), the MANEUVER 5 tri-fleet exercise in October

2013, the deployment of the PLA hospital ship to the Philippines for typhoon relief, Chinese participation in PEACE MISSION 2013 in July-August 2013, the goodwill voyage of the PLA Navy to South America, the first overseas demonstration of the PLA Air Force Aerobatics Team in Russia in August 2013, and Chinese participation in the Association of Southeast Asian Nations (ASEAN) Defense Minister's Meeting Plus (ADMM+) humanitarian assistance/disaster relief exercise in June 2013. The *PLA Daily* also highlighted China's November 2013 declaration of an Air Defense Identification Zone (ADIZ) in the East China Sea.

Combined Exercises. PLA participation in bilateral and multilateral exercises is increasing. The PLA derives political benefit through increased influence and enhanced ties with partner states and organizations. Such exercises provide the PLA opportunities to improve capabilities and gain operational insights by observing tactics, command, and equipment used by more advanced militaries.

In 2013, the PLA conducted seven bilateral and multilateral exercises with foreign militaries, three of which were with Russia. Other activities included military exercises with Shanghai Cooperation Organization (SCO) members, naval exercises, ground forces training, peacekeeping, and search-and-rescue operations and missions. The PLA Air Force (PLAAF) deployed FB-7A (JH-7A) multirole aircraft to Russia for PEACE MISSION 2013, which China referred to as an anti-terrorism exercise, and hosted

Pakistan Air Force fighters for SHAHEEN-II. China also conducted joint training for operations other than war. In 2013, the PLA sent its hospital ship and 110 engineers and medical officers to an HA/DR Military Medicine Joint Exercise under the auspices of the ASEAN Defense Ministers Meeting Plus" (ADMM+) in Brunei. The PLA Navy also conducted a goodwill tour to South America in 2013 from October until December aimed at improving relationships and HA/DR.

Peacekeeping Operations.

China continues to participate in United Nations (UN) peacekeeping operations (PKO) and maintains approximately 1,900 military observers and troops in 10 operations as of the end of 2013, mostly in sub-Saharan Africa and the Middle East. This level of support has been consistent since 2008 and is the highest among the permanent members of the UN Security Council. China is the sixth-largest financial contributor to the UN peacekeeping budget—fourth among Security Council members—pledging 6.64 percent of the total $7.54 billion budget for the period July 2013-July 2014.

Participation in peacekeeping operations serves various objectives, including improving China's international image, obtaining operational experience for the PLA, providing opportunities to gather intelligence, and advancing the PLA's "New Historic Missions" by taking on roles and generating capabilities for operations far beyond China's borders. China provides civilian police, military observers, engineers, logistics support, and medical troops to UN missions.

In 2012, China for the first time deployed an armed infantry unit to a UN peacekeeping operation. This "guard unit," as Chinese media described it, provides security for PLA engineering and medical personnel in the UN Mission in the Republic of South Sudan (UNMISS). These units, likely no more than 50 personnel from the 162nd Motorized Infantry Division, were equipped with armored vehicles, enabling them to provide fixed-site security and escort convoys. In late-2013, China deployed approximately 400 military personnel, which included a guard unit, as part of the Multidimensional Integrated Stabilization Mission in Mali (MINUSMA). Although China's contributions to UN peacekeeping operations thus far have been relatively limited, when compared to other nations, China will likely consider increasing its participation in future peacekeeping deployments.

Chinese Arms Sales.
From 2008 to 2012, China signed about $10 billion in agreements for conventional arms sales worldwide. China primarily conducts arms sales in conjunction with economic aid and development assistance to support broader foreign policy goals such as securing access to natural resources and export markets, promoting its political influence among host-country elites, and building support in international fora. To a lesser extent, arms sales also reflect the profit-seeking activities of individual arms

trading companies and offset some defense-related research and development costs.

From the perspective of China's arms customers (most of which are developing countries), Chinese arms are less expensive than those offered by the top international arms suppliers, although they are also generally of lower quality and reliability. Chinese arms also come with fewer political strings attached, which is attractive to those customers that may not have access to other sources of arms for political or economic reasons. China also offers relatively generous and flexible payment options to some customers.

Counterpiracy Efforts. China continues to support counterpiracy efforts in the Gulf of Aden, a commitment that began in December 2008. In July 2012, the PLA Navy deployed its twelfth escort formation, which included two guided missile frigates and one oiler, and these ships made a port call in Vietnam in January 2013 when returning to China. In April 2013, after its departure from the Gulf of Aden, the PLA Navy's thirteenth escort formation made port calls in Malta, Algeria, Morocco, Portugal, and France. In August 2013, the fourteenth escort formation participated in a joint counterpiracy exercise in the Gulf of Aden with the U.S. Navy. As of late December, the sixteenth escort formation had relieved the fifteenth escort formation, which subsequently conducted port visits in Africa before returning to China. The sixteenth escort formation assumed counterpiracy operations in the Gulf of Aden while one unit,

a JIANGKAI II guided missile frigate (FFG), repositioned into the Mediterranean to support the escort of ships transporting removed chemical weapons from Syria.

Territorial Disputes. Senior Chinese officials have identified protecting China's sovereignty and territorial integrity as a "core interest," and PRC officials repeatedly state China's opposition to actions they perceive as a challenge to this core interest.

In the South China Sea, Chinese maritime law enforcement vessels maintained a presence at Scarborough Reef throughout 2013, following the 2012 standoff with the Philippine coast guard. In May 2013, China sent maritime law enforcement ships to the waters near Second Thomas Shoal in the disputed Spratly Islands. Philippine military personnel are stationed on Second Thomas Shoal aboard a former U.S. tank-landing ship that was deliberately grounded there in 1999. Both sides claim sovereignty over Scarborough Reef and Second Thomas Shoal, and China maintains a continuous civilian maritime law enforcement presence at both locations.

The Chinese Government maintains that its maritime rights extend to virtually the entire South China Sea and often illustrates its claim using a "nine-dash line" that encompasses much of the South China Sea area. At the same time, China is ambiguous about the precise meaning of the nine-dash line. To date, China has not clarified the meaning of the line or articulated its legal basis. In January 2013, the Philippines requested arbitration from the UN Convention on the Law of the Sea

(UNCLOS) Commission to challenge China's nine-dash line claim. China has opted out of the proceedings.

As China increases activities in the South China Sea in support of its maritime claims, Chinese forces are interacting more frequently with other countries' forces. On December 5, 2013, a PLA Navy vessel and a U.S. Navy vessel operating in the South China Sea came into close proximity. At the time of the incident, USS COWPENS (CG 63) was operating approximately 32 nautical miles southeast of Hainan Island. In that location, the U.S. Navy vessel was conducting lawful military activities beyond the territorial sea of any coastal State, consistent with customary international law as reflected in the Law of the Sea Convention. Two PLA Navy vessels approached USS COWPENS. During this interaction, one of the PLA Navy vessels altered course and crossed directly in front of the bow of USS COWPENS. This maneuver by the PLA Navy vessel forced USS COWPENS to come to full stop to avoid collision, while the PLA Navy vessel passed less than 100 yards ahead. The PLA Navy vessel's action was inconsistent with internationally recognized rules concerning professional maritime behavior (i.e., the Convention of International Regulations for Preventing Collisions at Sea), to which China is a party.

In the East China Sea, China claims sovereignty over the Senkaku Islands, which the Chinese refer to as the Diaoyu Islands. The Senkaku Islands are under the administration of Japan and are also claimed by Taiwan. In April 2012, the Governor of Tokyo announced plans to purchase three of the five Senkaku Islands from private Japanese owners. In September 2012, the Government of Japan purchased the three islands. China protested the move and since that time has regularly sent maritime law enforcement ships – and, less often, aircraft – to patrol near the Senkaku Islands to assert PRC claims, including regular Chinese maritime operations within 12 nautical miles (nm) of the islands. In November 2013, China announced an Air Defense Identification Zone (ADIZ) in the East China Sea with coverage that included the Senkaku Islands and overlapped with previously established Japanese, South Korean and Taiwan zones.

China's East China Sea Air Defense Identification Zone (ADIZ)

On November 23, 2013, China announced the establishment of an ADIZ in the East China Sea. The newly announced ADIZ overlaps with territories administered by Japan as well as parts of the previously established and long-standing ADIZs of Japan, the Republic of Korea, and Taiwan. The United States neither accepts nor recognizes China's requirements for operating in the newly declared ADIZ. This announcement will not change how the United States conducts military operations in the region.

EAST CHINA SEA AIR DEFENSE IDENTIFICATION ZONES

THE SECURITY SITUATION IN THE TAIWAN STRAIT

Dealing with a potential contingency in the Taiwan Strait remains the PLA's primary mission despite an overall reduction of cross-Strait tensions—a trend that continued following the re-election of Taiwan President Ma Ying-jeou in January 2012. Should conditions change, the PLA could be called upon to compel Taiwan to abandon possible moves toward independence or to re-unify Taiwan with the mainland by force of arms while deterring or defeating any third-party intervention on Taiwan's behalf.

Cross-Strait Relations. In the months following China's 2012-2013 leadership transition, China does not appear to have fundamentally altered its approach to Taiwan. Both sides continue to explore ways to make progress on historically contentious issues. President Xi stated in October 2013 that, "the political divide that exists between the two sides must reach a final resolution step-by-step and cannot be passed from generation to generation." In return, Taiwan President Ma offered an "economics first, politics later" policy for dealing with the mainland, though the Taiwan legislature continues to debate the passage of a Trade in Services agreement with the mainland to further economic cooperation.

Despite occasional signs of impatience, China appears content to respect Taiwan's current approach to cross-Strait relations. In November 2012, China's President Xi sent a message to Taiwan's President Ma – in the latter's capacity as chairman of the ruling Kuomintang Party – emphasizing the need to continue promoting the peaceful development of cross-Strait relations. On February 11, 2014, Taiwan's Mainland Affairs Council Director Wang Yu-Chi and China's Taiwan Affairs Office Director Zhang Zhijun held a historic cross-Strait meeting in Nanjing, addressing each other by their official titles. The meeting focused on opening a cross-Strait communication channel, and the two leaders promised future meetings to discuss a broad range of cross-Strait issues.

CURRENT CAPABILITIES OF THE PEOPLE'S LIBERATION ARMY

Second Artillery Force. The Second Artillery controls most of China's nuclear and conventional ballistic missiles. It is developing and testing several new classes and variants of offensive missiles, forming additional missile units, upgrading older missile systems, and developing methods to counter ballistic missile defenses.

By November 2013, the Second Artillery possessed more than 1,000 short-range ballistic missiles (SRBMs) in its inventory. China is increasing the lethality of this missile force by fielding new conventional medium-range ballistic missiles (MRBMs) to improve its ability to strike not only Taiwan but other regional targets.

China is fielding a limited but growing number of conventionally armed medium-range ballistic missiles, including the CSS-5 Mod 5 (DF-21D) anti-ship ballistic missile (ASBM). The CSS-5 Mod 5 gives the PLA the capability to attack large ships, including aircraft carriers, in the western Pacific Ocean. The CSS-5 Mod 5 has a range exceeding 1,500 km and is armed with a maneuverable warhead.

The Second Artillery continues to modernize its nuclear forces by enhancing its silo-based intercontinental ballistic missiles (ICBMs) and adding more survivable mobile delivery systems. In recent years, the road-mobile, solid-propellant CSS-10 Mod 2 (DF-31A) ICBM has entered service. The CSS-10 Mod 2, with a range in excess of 11,200 km, can reach most locations within the continental United States. China also is developing a new road-mobile ICBM known as the Dong Feng-41 (DF-41), possibly capable of carrying multiple independently targetable re-entry vehicles (MIRV).

PLA Navy (PLAN). The PLA Navy has the largest force of major combatants, submarines, and amphibious warfare ships in Asia. China's naval forces include some 77 principal surface combatants, more than 60 submarines, 55 medium and large amphibious ships, and roughly 85 missile-equipped small combatants. The PLA Navy continues to expand its operational and deployment areas further into the Pacific and Indian Oceans. The October MANEUVER-5 exercise in the Philippine Sea, which included participation from all three PLAN fleets – the North Sea Fleet, the East Sea Fleet, and the South Sea Fleet – was the largest PLAN open-ocean exercise seen to date.

In 2013, the PLAN's first aircraft carrier, LIAONING (CV-16) shifted home ports from Dalian, where it was located since 2001, to the PLA Navy's Yuchi Naval Base, located in the North Sea Fleet. The LIAONING continued flight integration training throughout 2013, but it is not expected to embark an operational air wing until 2015 or later. In November 2013, the LIAONING deployed out of area for the first time to the South China Sea, where it conducted local training near Hainan Island with surface ships. China also continues to pursue an indigenous aircraft carrier program (the LIAONING is a refurbished ship, purchased from Ukraine in 1998) and likely will build multiple aircraft carriers over the next decade. The first Chinese-built carrier will likely be operational sometime at the beginning of the next decade.

The PLA Navy places a high priority on the modernization of its submarine force. China continues the production of JIN-class nuclear-powered ballistic missile submarines (SSBNs). Three JIN-class SSBNs (Type 094) are currently operational, and up to five may enter service before China proceeds to its next generation SSBN (Type 096) over the next decade. The JIN-class SSBN will carry the new JL-2 submarine-launched ballistic missile (SLBM) with an estimated range of 7,400 km. The JIN-class and the JL-2 will give the PLA Navy its first credible sea-based nuclear deterrent. China is likely to conduct its first nuclear deterrence patrols with the JIN-class SSBN in 2014.

China also has expanded its force of nuclear-powered attack submarines (SSNs). Two SHANG-class SSNs (Type 093) are already in service, and China is building four improved variants of the SHANG-class SSN, which will replace the aging HAN-class SSNs (Type 091). In the next decade, China likely will construct the Type 095 guided-missile attack submarine (SSGN), which may enable a submarine-based land-attack capability. In addition to likely incorporating better quieting technologies, the Type 095 will fulfill traditional anti-ship roles with the incorporation of torpedoes and anti-ship cruise missiles (ASCMs).

The mainstay of the Chinese submarine force remains the diesel-powered attack submarine (SS). In addition to twelve KILO-class submarines acquired from Russia in the 1990s and 2000s, eight of which are equipped with the SS-N-27 ASCM, the PLA Navy possesses 13 SONG-class SS (Type 039) and 12 YUAN-class SSP (Type 039A). The YUAN-class SSP is armed similarly to the SONG-class SS, but also includes a possible air-independent power system. China may plan to construct up to 20 YUAN-class SSPs.

Since 2008, the PLA Navy has embarked on a robust surface combatant construction program, including guided missile destroyers (DDGs) and guided missile frigates (FFGs). During 2013, China continued series production of several classes, including construction of a new generation DDG. Construction of the LUYANG II-class DDG (Type 052C) continued with three ships under various stages of construction and sea trials, which will bring the total number of ships of this class to six by 2015. Additionally, the first LUYANG III-class DDG (Type 052D), which will likely enter service in 2014, incorporates the PLA Navy's first multipurpose vertical launch system, likely capable of launching ASCMs, land-attack cruise missiles (LACMs), surface-to-air missiles (SAMs), and anti-submarine missiles. China is projected to build more than a dozen of these ships to replace the aging LUDA-class destroyers (DD). China has continued the construction of the workhorse JIANGKAI II-class FFG (Type 054A), with 15 ships currently in the fleet and five or more in various stages of construction, and yet more expected. These new DDGs and FFGs provide a significant upgrade to the PLA Navy's area air defense capability, which will be critical as it expands operations into "distant seas" beyond the range of shore-based air defenses.

To augment the PLA Navy's littoral warfare capabilities, especially in the South China Sea and East China Sea, China developed the

JIANGDAO-class corvette (FFLs) (Type 056). Nine corvettes entered service in 2013. China may build an additional 20 to 30 vessels of this class. These FFLs augment the 60 HOUBEI-class wave-piercing catamaran missile patrol boats (PTGs) (Type 022), each capable of carrying eight YJ-83 ASCMs, for operations in littoral waters. No significant amphibious construction was observed in 2013. However, it appears likely that China will build its first amphibious assault ship during this decade.

PLA Air Force (PLAAF). The PLAAF is the largest air force in Asia and the third-largest air force in the world, with approximately 330,000 personnel and more than 2,800 total aircraft, not including unmanned aerial vehicles (UAV). Of these PLAAF aircraft, approximately 1,900 are combat aircraft (includes fighters, bombers, fighter-attack and attack aircraft), 600 of which are modern. The PLAAF is pursuing modernization on a scale unprecedented in its history and is rapidly closing the gap with Western air forces across a broad spectrum of capabilities including aircraft, command and control (C2), jammers, electronic warfare (EW), and data links. Although it still operates a large number of older second- and third-generation fighters, it will likely become a majority fourth-generation force within the next several years.

To bolster its tactical air forces, China is attempting to procure the Su-35 advanced Flanker aircraft from Russia along with its advanced IRBIS-E passive electronically scanned array radar system. If China does procure the Su-35, these aircraft could enter service in 2016 or 2018.

China is also vigorously pursuing fifth-generation capabilities. Within two years of the J-20 stealth fighter's first flight in January 2011, China tested a second next-generation fighter prototype. The prototype, referred to as the J-31, is similar in size to a U.S. F-35 fighter and appears to incorporate design characteristics similar to the J-20. It conducted its first flight on October 31, 2012. At present, it is unclear if the J-31 is being developed for the PLAAF or the PLA Navy Air Force, or as an export platform to compete with the U.S. F-35.

China continues upgrading its H-6 bomber fleet, which was originally adapted from the late-1950s Soviet Tu-16 design, to increase operational effectiveness and lethality by integrating new stand-off weapons. China also uses a modified version of the H-6 aircraft for aerial refueling. The H-6G variant, in service with the PLA Navy Air Force, has four weapons pylons that are probably for ASCMs. China has developed the H-6K variant with new turbofan engines for extended range. It is believed to be capable of carrying six LACMs. Modernizing the H-6 into a cruise missile carrier has given the PLA Air Force a long-range stand-off offensive capability with precision-guided munitions.

The PLA Air Force possesses one of the largest forces of advanced SAM systems in the world, consisting of a combination of Russian-sourced SA-20 (S-300PMU1/2) battalions and domestically produced CSA-9 (HQ-9) battalions. China may become the first country to import Russia's S-400/Triumf SAM system as a follow-on to the SA-20, while simultaneously developing its indigenous HQ-19 which appears to be very similar to the S-400.

China's aviation industry is testing a large transport aircraft (referred to as the Y-20) to supplement China's fleet of strategic airlift assets, which currently consists of a limited number of Russian-made IL-76 aircraft. The Y-20 made its maiden flight during January 2013 and is reported to be using the same Russian engines as the IL-76. These heavy-lift transports are intended to support airborne C2, logistics, paradrop, aerial refueling, and reconnaissance operations, as well as humanitarian assistance/disaster relief missions.

PLA Ground Force. The PLA is investing heavily in its ground force, emphasizing the ability to deploy campaign-level forces across long distances quickly. This modernization is playing out with wide-scale restructuring of PLA ground forces that includes a more rapid, flexible special operations force equipped with advanced technology; improved army aviation units using helicopters armed with precision-guided munitions; and C2 capabilities with improved networks providing real-time data sharing within and between units. In addition, the PLA has focused its modernization efforts on transforming from a motorized to a mechanized force, as well as improving the ground force's armored, air defense, aviation, ground-air coordination, and electronic warfare capabilities. PLA ground forces have benefited from increased production of new equipment, including the Z-10 and Z-19 attack helicopters, and from new air defense equipment including the PLA ground force's first medium-range SAM, the CSA-16, as well as domestically produced CSA-15s (a copy of the Russian SA-15) and a new advanced self-propelled air defense artillery system, the PGZ-07.

Space and Counterspace Capabilities. In 2013, China conducted at least eight space launches to expand its space-based intelligence, surveillance, reconnaissance, meteorological, and communications satellite constellations. In addition to expanding its in-orbit assets, China successfully launched its first "Kuaizhou" ("quick vessel") space launch vehicle (SLV), which is designed to launch a small satellite of the same name quickly into a low-Earth orbit to support "natural disaster monitoring." Chinese media also reported development of a second Chinese responsive space launch vehicle dubbed the Long March 11 (LM-11). The LM-11 will provide China with "a vehicle to rapidly enter space and meet the emergency launching demand in case of disasters and contingencies," and could be launched as early as 2014 and no later than 2016. In parallel, China is developing a multi-dimensional program to improve its capabilities to limit or prevent the use of space-based assets by adversaries during times of crisis or conflict.

During 2013, China focused on testing the current constellation of Beidou navigation satellites (NAVSATs) and released the Beidou signal interface control document to allow for the production of ground receivers. Beidou NAVSAT launches will likely resume in 2014, with a global NAVSAT constellation expected to be completed by 2020. China launched five new remote sensing satellites in 2013, which can perform both civil and military applications. China also launched one communications satellite, four experimental small satellites, one meteorological satellite, and one manned space mission.

China continues to develop the LM-5 SLV, designed for lifting heavy payloads into space. The LM-5 will more than double the size of payloads China may place into geosynchronous orbits. More than just a single heavy-lift launch vehicle, the LM-5 has propulsion technologies that are reconfigurable to produce the LM-6 light-lift- and LM-7 medium-lift launch vehicles. The Wenchang Satellite Launch Center, designed to host these new launch vehicles, is expected to be complete in time for the first LM-7 launch in late-2014. The first LM-5 launch,

delayed by recent manufacturing difficulties, is expected no sooner than 2015.

Chinese Engagement on International Cyber Issues. China has increased diplomatic engagement and advocacy in multilateral and international fora where cyber issues are discussed and debated. China's agenda is frequently in line with Russia's efforts to promote more intergovernmental control over cyberspace. China and Russia continue to promote an Information Security Code of Conduct that advances a state-centric concept of cyberspace and seeks to impose state control of content in cyberspace. Given the growing consensus on the need for cyber transparency and confidence-building measures in international fora such as the ASEAN Regional Forum and the UN Group of Governmental Experts on Developments in the Field of Information and Telecommunications in the Context of International Security (UN GGE), China may be willing to play a more constructive role in these efforts. Notably, in June 2013, China joined a landmark consensus of the UN GGE that addressed three fundamental issues: (1) confirmed that existing international law, including the UN Charter, applies to cyberspace and that the law of state responsibility should guide state behavior with regard to the use of cyberspace; (2) expressed the need to promote international stability, transparency, and confidence in cyberspace; and (3) explored how the international community can help build the cybersecurity capacity of less-developed states.

DEVELOPMENTS IN CHINESE MILITARY DOCTRINE AND TRAINING

In 2013, the PLA emphasized training under "realistic combat scenarios" and the ability to execute long-range mobility operations. This type of training was highlighted by the MISSION ACTION 2013 series of exercises and the MANEUVER 5 PLA Navy exercise involving all three PLA Navy fleets. MISSION ACTION 2013 was a multi-week exercise led by the Nanjing and Guangzhou Military Regions (MRs) and the PLA Air Force. The exercise emphasized multiple PLA objectives including long-distance mobility and logistics, joint air-ground, and joint air-naval operations under realistic, high-tech conditions, and a series of amphibious landing operations.

Almost all of the PLA's 2013 exercises focused on operating in "informationized" conditions by emphasizing system-of-systems operations, a concept that can be viewed as the Chinese corollary to U.S. network-centric warfare. This concept requires enhancing systems and weapons with information capabilities and linking geographically dispersed forces and capabilities into an integrated system capable of unified action. These operational training reforms are a result of the Outline of Military Training and Evaluation (OMTE), which was last published in mid-2008 and became standard across the PLA on January 1, 2009. Since that time, the PLA has pushed to achieve OMTE objectives by emphasizing realistic training conditions, training in complex electromagnetic and joint environments, and integrating new technologies into the PLA force structure.

A result of these changes is a more flexible year-round training cycle, which is a departure from the Soviet-style conscript-dependent training cycles that were prominent throughout the PLA in previous decades. During 2013, the PLA continued its push toward year-round military training and aligned its recruiting cycle with China's post-secondary academic calendar to attract better educated recruits. The recruiting period now begins in August rather than October.

Additionally, the PLA is laying the foundation for future changes in military doctrine. To develop a new cadre of officers, the PLA is reshuffling its academies to cultivate junior officers proficient with and capable of leveraging technology in all warfighting functions for joint operations. The National University of Defense Technology, for example, launched a yearlong joint operations staff officer course to serve as a pilot for a future national-level program. The course allows junior officers to rotate to the command elements of other PLA services to enhance their skills in joint operations planning and preparation.

ADVANCED TECHNOLOGY ACQUISITION

China relies on foreign technology, acquisition of key dual-use components, and focused indigenous research and development (R&D) to advance military modernization. Many of the organizations in China's military-industrial complex have both military and civilian R&D functions. This network of government-affiliated companies and research institutes often provides the PLA access to sensitive and dual-use technologies or knowledgeable experts under the guise of civilian R&D. The enterprises and institutes accomplish this through technology conferences and symposia, legitimate contracts and joint commercial ventures, partnerships with foreign firms, and joint development of specific technologies. In the case of key national security technologies, controlled equipment, and other materials not readily obtainable through commercial means or academia, China has used its intelligence services and other illicit approaches to collect sensitive U.S. information and export-controlled technology in violation of U.S. laws and export controls.

A high priority for China's advanced technology acquisition strategy is its civil-military integration policy to develop an innovative dual-use technology and industrial base that serve both military and civilian requirements. China's defense industry has benefited from integration with its expanding civilian economy and science and technology sectors, particularly sectors with access to foreign technology. Examples of technologies include advanced aviation and aerospace (hot section technologies, avionics, and flight controls), source code, traveling wave tubes, night vision devices, monolithic microwave integrated circuits, and information and cyber technologies.

Differentiating between China's civil and military end-use remains a challenge due to opaque corporate structures, hidden asset ownership, and the connections of commercial personnel with the central government. Some commercial entities are affiliated with PLA research institutes or have ties to and are subject to the control of government organizations such as the State-Owned Assets Supervision and Administration Commission.

2

UNDERSTANDING CHINA'S STRATEGY

NATIONAL LEVEL PRIORITIES AND GOALS

Since 2002, China's leaders have described the initial two decades of the 21st century as a "period of strategic opportunity." They assess that during this time, international conditions will be conducive to domestic development and expanding China's "comprehensive national power," a term that encapsulates all elements of state power, including economic capacity, military might, and diplomacy. China's leaders anticipate that a successful expansion of comprehensive national power will serve China's overriding strategic objectives, which include perpetuating Chinese Communist Party (CCP) rule, sustaining economic growth and development, maintaining domestic political stability, defending national sovereignty and territorial integrity, and securing China's status as a great power. Though there is debate in Chinese academic circles over whether China can sustain the "period of strategic opportunity" though this decade, Chinese leaders have continued to reiterate the centrality of this period to achieving these key strategic objectives.

China's leaders routinely emphasize the goal of reaching critical economic and military benchmarks by 2020. These benchmarks include successfully restructuring the economy to maintain growth and increase Chinese citizens' quality of life to promote stability; making major progress in military modernization; and, attaining the capability to fight and win potential regional conflicts, including those related to Taiwan, protection of sea lines of communication (SLOCs), defense of territorial claims in the South China Sea and East China Sea, and defense of western borders. Statements by Chinese leaders indicate that, in their view, the development of a modern military is necessary for China to achieve great power status. These statements also indicate that the Chinese leadership views a modern military as a deterrent to prevent adversaries from threatening Chinese interests or to allow China to defend itself, should deterrence fail.

Since China launched its "reform and opening" in late 1978, the essential elements of China's strategy to accomplish these goals have remained relatively constant. Chinese leaders have adopted a pragmatic approach to international relations and economic development that seeks to strengthen the economy, modernize the military, and solidify the CCP's hold on power. China's leaders routinely reassure neighboring countries that its rise is peaceful while simultaneously taking steps to strengthen control over existing sovereignty and territorial claims.

China regards stable relations with its neighbors and the United States as essential to stability and development. China continues to see the United States as the dominant regional and global actor with the greatest potential to both support, and potentially disrupt, China's rise. Many Chinese officials and citizens argue that the U.S. strategy to rebalance to the Asia-Pacific region is further proof of "Cold War thinking" and a U.S. effort to "contain" China's rise. In addition, Chinese leaders have expressed concerns that should regional states come to view China as a threat, they may seek to deepen their relationships with the United States.

Despite China's desire to project the image of a benign developing country, its efforts to defend "national sovereignty and territorial integrity," underpinned by growing economic strength and military capabilities, have been manifest in more forceful rhetoric and confrontational behavior in recent years. Prominent examples of this behavior include: China's response to Japan's arrest of a PRC fishing trawler captain following a collision with Japanese coast guard vessels in 2010;

China's use of punitive trade policies as an instrument of coercion; and China's actions to pressure Vietnam and the Philippines in the South China Sea and Japan in the East China Sea. Official statements and media during these situations seek to frame China as reacting to threats to its national interests or provocations by outside actors. China's lack of transparency surrounding its growing military capabilities and strategic decision-making has led to increased concerns in the region about China's intentions. Absent greater transparency from China and a change in its behavior, these concerns will likely intensify as the PLA's military modernization program progresses.

Fulfilling the "New Historic Missions"

The PLA's "New Historic Missions"—first articulated by then-President Hu Jintao in 2004 and codified in a 2007 amendment to the Chinese Communist Party (CCP) Constitution—have guided the PLA's modernization and foreign engagement efforts for almost a decade. The missions were largely driven by a desire to realign the PLA's tasks with the CCP's strategic objectives and still reflect the leadership's view of China's security situation. The missions include:

- Provide an important guarantee of strength for the CCP to consolidate its ruling position.

- Provide a strong security guarantee for safeguarding the period of strategic opportunity for national development.

- Provide a powerful strategic support for safeguarding national interests.

- Play an important role in safeguarding world peace and promoting common development.

The PLA has adopted these imperatives and put them into practice over the past decade, particularly its role as guarantor of the CCP's ruling position. This has been critical to maintaining stability during China's leadership transition, important CCP meetings, and various corruption scandals among senior officials in 2013. The PLA has implemented the other missions through continued modernization and professionalization focused on protecting China's national interests and sovereignty claims. It has also taken on a larger role in military diplomacy, peacekeeping, and humanitarian aid/disaster relief operations. President Xi's instructions to the PLA to resolutely obey the CCP while preparing to "fight and win battles" were clearly broadcast throughout the force in 2013.

FACTORS SHAPING CHINA'S LEADERSHIP PERCEPTIONS

Following China's once-in-a-decade leadership turnover, bookended by the Eighteenth Party Congress in fall 2012 and the National People's Congress in spring 2013, China's new leader, Xi Jinping, assumed the top Party, State, and military posts from his predecessor Hu Jintao. In addition, China named a new Premier and Defense Minister. This new generation of Chinese leaders continues to view itself as operating in a "period of strategic opportunity" to advance the priorities of economic development, territorial integrity, and domestic stability. Despite offering a generally positive view of China's strategic environment, official documents indicate that China sees its security environment as more complex as a result of several evolving factors:

Economics. Chinese leaders believe continued, robust economic development remains the bedrock of social stability. A wide range of economic factors could disrupt this trajectory, including a failure to shift away from China's overreliance on investment and exports to drive growth. China's leaders scaled back Gross Domestic Product (GDP) targets for 2011-2015 to mitigate risk of overheating the economy and to manage expectations. Other potential economic risks for China include shifting global trade patterns, domestic resource constraints, rising wages driven by labor shortages, and reduced access to global resources, including energy. China is experimenting with a new free trade zone in Shanghai, and additional structural reforms to China's economy were announced at the CCP Third Plenum in November 2013.

Nationalism. Communist Party leaders and military officials continue to exploit nationalism to bolster the legitimacy of the Party, deflect domestic criticism, and justify their own inflexibility in dialogues with foreign interlocutors. However, nationalism also constrains the leadership's decision-making on key policy issues, particularly with respect to foreign security policy.

Regional Challenges to China's Interests. Ongoing tensions with Japan in the East China Sea and with a number of Southeast Asian nations in the South China Sea complicate China's desire to maintain a stable periphery. Combined with greater U.S. presence in the region, these factors raise Chinese concerns that regional countries will strengthen their military capabilities or increase security cooperation with the United States to counterbalance China.

Domestic Unrest. The CCP continues to face long-term popular demands to eradicate corruption and improve government responsiveness to citizens' demands, as well as greater transparency and accountability. Unmet demands could threaten CCP legitimacy. A national anti-corruption campaign is underway in part to address public concerns.

Environment. China's economic development has come at a high environmental cost. China's leaders are increasingly concerned that environmental degradation could undermine regime legitimacy by threatening economic development, public health, social stability, and China's international image.

Demographics. China faces the dual threat of a rapidly aging population and a declining birth rate, one that now falls below replacement level. Longer life expectancies may force China to allocate more resources to social and health services, while the declining birth rate will continue to reduce China's supply of young and inexpensive labor, a key driver of the country's three decades of economic growth. This dual phenomenon could lead to economic stagnation that could threaten CCP legitimacy.

China's Energy Strategy

China's engagement, investment, and foreign construction related to energy continue to grow. China has constructed or invested in energy projects in more than 50 countries, spanning nearly every continent. This ambitious investment in energy assets is driven primarily by two factors. First, China is increasingly dependent upon imported energy to sustain its economy. A net oil exporter until 1993, China remains suspicious of international energy markets. Second, energy projects present a viable option for investing China's vast foreign currency holdings.

In addition to ensuring reliable energy sources, China hopes to diversify both producers and transport options. Although energy independence is no longer realistic for China, given population growth and increasing per capita energy consumption, China still seeks to maintain a supply chain that is less susceptible to external disruption.

In 2012, China imported approximately 60 percent of its oil; conservative estimates project that China will import almost two-thirds of its oil by 2015 and three-quarters by 2030. China looks primarily to the Persian Gulf, Africa, and Russia/Central Asia to satisfy its growing demand, with imported oil accounting for approximately 11 percent of China's total energy consumption.

A second goal of China's foreign energy strategy is to alleviate China's heavy dependence on Sea Lines of Communication (SLOCs), particularly the South China Sea and Strait of Malacca. In 2012, approximately 84 percent of China's oil imports transited the South China Sea and Strait of Malacca. Separate crude oil pipelines from Russia and Kazakhstan to China illustrate efforts to increase overland supply. In 2013, Chinese and Russian oil companies were in the late stages of negotiations to double the capacity of the crude oil pipeline that delivers Russian crude oil to China from 300,000 barrels per day (b/d) to 600,000 b/d. A pipeline that would bypass the Strait of Malacca by transporting crude oil from Kyuakpya, Burma, to Kunming, China, was completed in 2013 and is expected to commence operations in 2014. The crude oil for this pipeline will be supplied by Saudi Arabia and other countries in the Middle East and Africa.

Given China's growing energy demand, new pipelines will only slightly alleviate China's maritime dependency on either the Strait of Malacca or the Strait of Hormuz. Despite China's efforts, the sheer volume of oil and liquefied natural gas that is imported to China from the Middle East and Africa will make strategic SLOCs increasingly important to China.

In 2012, China imported 21.3 billion cubic meters (bcm) of natural gas, or 51 percent of all of its natural gas imports, from Turkmenistan to China by pipeline via Kazakhstan and Uzbekistan. This pipeline is designed to carry 40 bcm per year with plans to expand it to 60 bcm. Another natural gas pipeline designed to deliver 12 bcm per year of Burmese-produced gas was completed in 2013 and is estimated to commence operations in 2014. This pipeline parallels the crude oil pipeline across Burma. China is in the late stages of negotiations with Russia for two pipelines that could supply China with up to 68 bcm of gas per year. In 2012, China imported about 25 percent of its gas supply.

China's Top Crude Suppliers 2012

Country	Volume (1,000 barrels/day	Percentage of Imported Crude Oil
Saudi Arabia	1,100	20
Angola	806	15
Russia	489	9
Iran	442	8
Oman	393	7
Iraq	315	6
Venezuela	307	6
Kazakhstan	215	4
Kuwait	211	4
UAE	176	3
Others	990	18
Total	**5,444**	**100**

INTERNAL DEBATE OVER CHINA'S REGIONAL AND GLOBAL ROLE

China's leadership continues to support former paramount leader Deng Xiaoping's dictum from the early-1990s that China should "observe calmly; secure our position; cope with affairs calmly; hide our capabilities and bide our time; be good at maintaining a low profile; and never claim leadership." This guidance reflected Deng's belief that Chinese interests are best served by focusing on internal development and stability while steering clear of direct confrontation or antagonism with major powers. In December 2010, then-State Councilor Dai Bingguo specifically cited Deng's guidance, insisting China adhered to a "path of peaceful development" and would not seek expansion or hegemony. He asserted that the "hide and bide" rhetoric was not a "smokescreen" employed while China builds its strength, but rather an admonition to be patient and not stand out.

However, some Chinese scholars debate whether Deng's policy approach will continue to win support as China's interests increase abroad and its power expands. China's perceived security interests have changed considerably since Deng's era to include a heavy reliance on maritime commerce. China's improving naval capabilities enable roles and missions that would have been impossible for the PLA to pursue just a decade ago. Proponents of a more active Chinese role on the world stage have suggested that China would be better served by a firm stance in the face of U.S. or other regional pressure. These voices could increase as a result of renewed tensions since 2012 with the Philippines and Vietnam over the South China Sea and with Japan over the Senkaku Islands.

China's Periphery. The Chinese leadership faces a policy dilemma in seeking to maintain a stable periphery in order to ensure that its "period of strategic opportunity" for development remains open. China also perceives other regional countries are asserting their national interests along China's periphery and feels compelled to respond to ensure continued stability. However, China's leaders are concerned that too strong of a response may motivate regional actors to counterbalance China's rise through greater cooperation with each other and the United States. Therefore, China's leaders are trying to maintain a delicate balance between defending territorial integrity in the face of what it perceives as growing provocations by its neighbors, while concurrently tamping down threat perceptions across the globe. China publicly states that its rise is "peaceful" and that it harbors no "hegemonic" designs or aspirations for territorial expansion. However, China's lack of transparency surrounding its growing military capabilities has increased concerns in the region about China's intentions.

China's Territorial Disputes

China's use of force in territorial disputes – both on land and at sea – has varied throughout history. Some disputes led to armed conflict, such as China's border conflicts with India in 1962 and Vietnam in 1979. A contested border with the former Soviet Union during the 1960s raised the possibility of nuclear war. In more recent cases, China has been willing to compromise with and even offer concessions to its neighbors. Since 1998, China has settled eleven land-based territorial disputes with six of its neighbors. In China's maritime periphery, tensions continue over exclusive economic zones (EEZs) and ownership of potentially rich, off-shore oil and gas deposits.

The East China Sea contains approximately seven trillion cubic feet of natural gas and up to 100 billion barrels of oil. Japan maintains that an equidistant line from each country should separate the EEZs, while China claims an extended continental shelf beyond the equidistant line to the Okinawa Trench (which almost reaches Japan's shore). In early 2009, Japan accused China of violating a June 2008 agreement providing for joint exploration of oil and natural gas fields and claimed that China unilaterally drilled beneath the demarcation line, extracting reserves from the Japanese side. China continues to contest Japan's administrative control of the Senkaku Islands to the south.

The South China Sea plays an important role in Northeast and Southeast Asian security considerations. Northeast Asia relies heavily on the flow of oil and commerce through South China Sea shipping lanes, including more than 80 percent of the crude oil to Japan, South Korea, and Taiwan. China claims sovereignty over the Spratly and Paracel Island groups and other land formations within its "nine-dash line" claim—parts of which are disputed in whole or in part by Brunei, the Philippines, Malaysia, Indonesia, and Vietnam. Taiwan, which occupies Itu Aba in the Spratly Islands among other features, makes the same claims as China. In 2009, China protested extended continental shelf claims in the South China Sea made by Malaysia and Vietnam. In its protest to the UN Commission, China included the ambiguous "nine-dash line" and reiterated that it has "indisputable sovereignty over the islands in the South China Sea and the adjacent waters and enjoys sovereign rights and jurisdiction over the relevant waters as well as the seabed and subsoil thereof."

Despite improving political and economic relations between China and India, tensions remain along their shared 4,057-km border, most notably over Arunachal Pradesh (which China asserts is part of Tibet and therefore of China) and over the Aksai Chin region at the western end of the Tibetan Plateau. In 2009, China and India said they would establish a hotline between their Prime Ministers after exchanging barbs over the status of the border region of Arunachal Pradesh. By 2011, however, progress still lagged as India reportedly found trouble obtaining suitable encryption technology to establish the hotline. Chinese and Indian officials met in late September 2013 to finalize the text of the Border Defense Cooperation Agreement, which will supplement existing procedures managing the interaction of troops along the Line of Actual Control.

Power Projection Capability. There also has been an active debate among military and civilian theorists in China concerning future capabilities the PLA should develop to advance China's interests beyond traditional requirements. Some senior officers and civilian theorists advocate an expansion of the PLA's power projection capabilities to facilitate missions well beyond Taiwan and regional disputes. Publicly, Chinese officials contend that increasing the scope of China's maritime capabilities is intended to build capacity for international peacekeeping, humanitarian assistance, disaster relief, and protection of sea lanes. The commissioning of the PLA Navy's first aircraft carrier in 2012, in addition to serving as a symbol of national prestige, exemplifies these aspirations.

Indicators of Decision and Intent. There are several possible indicators of change in Chinese decision-making or intentions, depending on the issue. This could be reflected through speeches in regional and multi-national organizations, commentary in official domestic newspapers or prominent Chinese think tanks, adjustments to CCP reports or China's Defense White Paper, changes in talking points with civilian and military interlocutors, disposition of forces, and changes in military diplomacy. The deployment, testing, and movement of military forces are the most concerning aspects of indications and warning, and it is unclear how China views the potentially escalatory nature of force posture.

PLA Military Engagement

The PLA's level of engagement with foreign militaries continues to grow. At the operational level, this engagement provides the PLA opportunities to share doctrine, strategies, tactics, techniques, and procedures with other militaries—both modern and developing. At the strategic level, China uses military engagement as a platform for demonstrating the PLA's growing capabilities, its status as a modern military, and its potential as a security partner.

Senior-level visits and exchanges provide China opportunities to increase military officers' international exposure, communicate China's positions to foreign audiences, better understand alternative world views, and advance foreign relations through interpersonal contacts and military assistance programs. Expanded PLA travel abroad enables China's military officers to observe and study foreign military command structures, unit formations, and operational training.

The PLA is participating in a growing number of bilateral and multilateral military exercises. The PLA derives political benefit from these exercises through increased influence and enhanced ties with partner States and organizations. These exercises also contribute to PLA modernization by providing opportunities to improve capabilities in areas such as counterterrorism, mobility operations, and logistics. The PLA gains operational insight by observing tactics, command and control, and equipment used by more advanced militaries. PLA participation or observation of military training and exercises with the United States or states in possession of U.S. military equipment, systems, and weapons is overseen by the Office of the Secretary of Defense to ensure compliance with applicable U.S. laws related to the transfer or disclosure of U.S.-origin defense articles, defense services, technical data, and/or technology to China. As China's regional and international interests grow more complex, the PLA's international engagement will expand, especially in the areas of peacekeeping operations, counterpiracy, humanitarian assistance/disaster relief, and joint exercises.

The strategic-level College of Defense Studies at PRC's National Defense University in Beijing welcomes officers from most Latin American and Caribbean countries that diplomatically recognize China, and some of those countries also send officers to the PLA and PLA Navy command schools in Nanjing. In addition to furthering PLA modernization, the focus of these engagements will likely remain on building China's political ties, assuaging fears about China's rise, and building China's international influence, particularly in Asia and Latin America.

China's Military Leadership

The PLA is the armed instrument of the CCP and organizationally is subordinate to the Party apparatus. Career military officers are CCP members, and units at the company level and above have political officers responsible for personnel decisions, propaganda, and counterintelligence. Major decisions at all levels are made by CCP committees, also led by the political officers and commanders.

The military's highest decision-making body, the Central Military Commission (CMC), is technically a department of the CCP Central Committee, but it is staffed almost exclusively by military officers. The CMC Chairman is a civilian, usually serving concurrently as the General Secretary of the CCP and President. Other members include several vice chairmen, the commanders of the services, and the directors of the four general headquarters departments. China's Ministry of National Defense (MND) is not equivalent to the "defense ministry" in most other nations, but rather is a small office coordinating military-related tasks where responsibility overlaps between the civilian government and the armed forces, including foreign military relations, mobilization, recruitment, "national defense education," and civil support to military operations. The Minister of Defense is a uniformed military officer, a member of the State Council (the country's chief administrative authority), and also a CMC member.

The PLA is an influential player in China's defense and foreign policy due to the CMC's special bureaucratic status and the PLA's near monopoly on military expertise. Even as the PLA remains subordinate to top Party leadership direction as the armed wing of the CCP, long-standing bureaucratic coordination issues and China's increasingly active media landscape have sometimes led to PLA-associated actions or statements that appear to diverge from the positions of China's other key bureaucratic actors, especially on national sovereignty or territorial issues.

Members of the Chinese Communist Party's Central Military Commission (CMC)

Chairman Xi Jinping's appointment as Party General Secretary, CMC Chairman, and State President over the course five months from late-2012 to early-2013 was a departure from the precedent set during Hu Jintao's appointments ten years earlier, when the assumption of all three titles took more than a year. Prior to the 2012-2013 leadership transition, Xi served as the CMC's only civilian Vice Chairman. Xi's father was an important military figure during the Chinese communist revolution and a Politburo member in the 1980s. The younger Xi served as secretary to a defense minister early in his career and would have had ample opportunities to interact with the PLA as a provincial Party official. In meetings with U.S. officials, Xi has emphasized increasing mutual trust between China and the United States.

Vice Chairman Fan Changlong is China's top uniformed officer. He formerly commanded the Jinan Military Region, a test bed for new operational concepts and technology that has been at the forefront of the PLA's joint training efforts in recent years. Fan was the longest-serving of China's seven Military Region commanders at the time of his promotion to the CMC. He spent 35 years in the Shenyang Military Region, adjacent to North Korea and Russia.

Vice Chairman Xu Qiliang—the first career air force officer promoted to CMC vice chairman—previously served on the CMC as PLAAF Commander where he oversaw rapid force modernization and expanded the air force's foreign engagement. Xu was the first PLAAF officer to serve as deputy chief of the General Staff Department (GSD) since the Cultural Revolution period and, at 54 years old, the youngest in PLA history.

Minister of National Defense Chang Wanquan was appointed to his current position at the National People's Congress in March 2013. The Minister of National Defense is the PLA's third most senior officer and manages the PLA's relationship with state bureaucracies and foreign militaries. Chang previously oversaw the PLA's weapons development and space portfolio as head of the General Armament Department. He is a veteran of China's border skirmishes with Vietnam and held top posts across military regions.

Chief of the General Staff Department Fang Fenghui oversees PLA operations, training, and intelligence. He served as "commander in chief" of China's 60th anniversary military parade in 2009 and oversaw security for the 2008 Beijing Olympic Games. Fang is the first Beijing Military Region commander to move directly to Chief of the General Staff Department. He was the youngest military region commander when he was promoted to lead the Beijing Military Region in 2007.

General Political Department Director Zhang Yang oversees the PLA's political work, including propaganda, discipline, and education. He previously served as Political Commissar of the Guangzhou Military Region, which borders Vietnam and the South China Sea. Zhang assumed that position at a relatively young age and is unusual among the other newly appointed CMC members for spending his entire career in one military region. Zhang participated in China's border conflict with Vietnam and supported disaster relief efforts following a January 2008 snowstorm in southern China.

General Logistics Department Director Zhao Keshi is responsible for overseeing PLA support functions, including finances, land, mining, and construction. Zhao spent his entire career in the Nanjing Military Region, which is responsible for PLA operations in a Taiwan contingency, and he most recently served as its Commander. He was reportedly an exercise commander in the large military drills that induced the 1996 Taiwan Strait Crisis. Zhao has written on defense mobilization and reserve construction.

General Armament Department Director Zhang Youxia is responsible for overseeing the military's weapons development and space program. Nicknamed "General Patton," he has rare experience as a combat commander during China's brief conflict with Vietnam in 1979. Zhang formerly commanded the Shenyang Military Region, which shares a border with North Korea and Russia. Zhang is one of China's military "princelings." His father, a well-known military figure in China, served with Xi Jinping's father in the 1940s.

PLA Navy Commander Wu Shengli has served as head of the navy since 2006 and has been a member of the CMC since 2007—only the second PLA Navy Commander to be a CMC member in recent decades. Under Wu, the navy has increased its out-of-area exercises, multinational patrols, and foreign naval exchanges and initiated its first deployment to the Gulf of Aden. The first career navy officer to serve as a Deputy Chief of the General Staff, Wu held leadership positions in two of the PLA Navy's three fleets, spending most of his career in the East Sea Fleet.

PLA Air Force Commander Ma Xiaotian previously oversaw the PLA's military engagement activities as a Deputy Chief of the General Staff. Ma led the PLA side in key military-to-military exchanges with the United States, including the Defense Consultative Talks and the Strategic Security Dialogue component of the U.S.-China Strategic and Economic Dialogue. Ma has significant operational experience both as a pilot and staff officer in multiple military regions.

Second Artillery Commander Wei Fenghe oversees China's strategic missile forces and bases. Wei served in multiple missile bases across different military regions and held top posts in the Second Artillery headquarters before being promoted in late 2010 to Deputy Chief of the General Staff – the first officer from the Second Artillery to do so. In that role, Wei met frequently with foreign delegations, including senior U.S. officials, affording him greater international exposure than previous Second Artillery commanders.

3

FORCE MODERNIZATION GOALS AND TRENDS

Although preparing for potential conflict in the Taiwan Strait remains the focus and primary driver of China's military modernization program, steadily increasing tensions in the East China and South China Seas, along with growing interests and influence abroad, have caused a substantial uptick in the PLA's preparations for a range of missions beyond China's immediate periphery.

China is investing in military programs and weapons designed to improve extended-range power projection and operations in emerging domains such as cyberspace, space, and electronic warfare. Current trends in China's weapons production will enable the PLA to conduct a range of military operations in Asia well beyond China's traditional territorial claims. Key systems that either have been deployed or are in development include ballistic missiles (including anti-ship variants), anti-ship and land-attack cruise missiles, nuclear submarines, modern surface ships, and an aircraft carrier. The need to ensure trade, particularly oil supplies from the Middle East, has prompted the PLA Navy to join international counterpiracy operations in the Gulf of Aden. Tensions with Japan over maritime claims in the East China Sea and with several Southeast Asian claimants to all or parts of the Spratly and Paracel Islands in the South China Sea have increased. In the coming years, instability on the Korean Peninsula could produce a regional crisis involving China's military. The desire to protect energy investments in Central Asia, along with potential security implications from cross-border support to ethnic separatists, could provide an incentive for military investment or intervention in this region if instability surfaces.

In addition to developing new capabilities to protect security and energy interests regionally, China's political leaders have charged the PLA with developing capabilities for missions in non-traditional security areas, such as peacekeeping, humanitarian assistance/disaster relief, and counterterrorism operations. Then-President Hu Jintao's 2004 announcement of the PLA's "New Historic Missions," for example, promoted: increased PRC participation in UN peacekeeping missions; greater PLA involvement in humanitarian assistance/disaster relief exercises; deployment of China's ANWEI-class military hospital ship (the PEACE ARK) throughout East Asia and to the Caribbean; PLA participation in four joint military exercises with SCO members, the most prominent being the PEACE MISSION series, with China and Russia as the main participants; and China's continued counterpiracy deployments to the Gulf of Aden that began in December 2008.

China refers to these new missions to message its aspirations for a global leadership role and to garner international respect. At the same time, these non-traditional missions likely serve as a key testing ground for the PLA: the experience gained and problems overcome on these missions will improve the operation of new capabilities in traditional security missions as well. The new capabilities may also increase China's options for military influence to press its diplomatic agenda, advance regional and international interests, and resolve disputes in China's favor.

PLA CAPABILITIES IN DEVELOPMENT

Nuclear Weapons. China officially maintains a No First Use (NFU) nuclear weapons policy in which it proclaims it will never be the first to use nuclear weapons in a conflict, will not threaten to use nuclear weapons against non-nuclear weapons states or nuclear weapons free zones, and will maintain a second-strike capability in order to retaliate after being attacked by nuclear weapons. However, there is some ambiguity over the conditions under which China's NFU policy would apply, including whether strikes on what China considers its own territory, demonstration strikes, or high-altitude bursts would constitute a first use. Moreover, some PLA officers have written publicly of the need to spell out conditions under which China might need to use nuclear weapons first. For example, if an enemy's conventional attack threatened the survival of China's nuclear force or the regime itself. However, there has been no indication that national leaders are willing to attach such nuances and caveats to China's NFU doctrine.

China's new generation of mobile missiles, with payloads consisting of Multiple Independently Targeted Reentry Vehicles (MIRVs) and penetration aids, are intended to ensure the viability of China's strategic deterrent in the face of continued advances in U.S. and, to a lesser extent, Russian strategic ISR, precision strike, and missile defense capabilities. The PLA has deployed new command, control, and communications capabilities to its nuclear forces. These capabilities improve the Second Artillery's ability to command and control multiple units in the field. Through the use of improved communications links, China's ICBM units now have better access to battlefield information and uninterrupted communications connecting all command echelons, and unit commanders are able to issue orders to multiple subordinates at once, instead of serially, via voice commands.

China will likely continue to invest considerable resources to maintain a limited, survivable, nuclear force (sometimes described as "sufficient and effective") to ensure the PLA can deliver a damaging retaliatory nuclear strike.

Land-Based Platforms. China's nuclear arsenal currently consists of the silo-based CSS-4 (DF-5); the solid-fueled, road-mobile CSS-10 Mod 1 and Mod 2 (DF-31 and DF-31A); and the more limited-range CSS-3 (DF-4). This force is complemented by road-mobile, solid-fueled CSS-5 (DF-21) MRBMs for regional deterrence missions. By 2015, China's nuclear forces will include additional CSS-10 Mod 2s.

PLA Underground Facilities

China maintains a technologically advanced underground facility (UGF) program protecting all aspects of its military forces, including command and control, logistics, and missile and naval forces. Given China's NFU nuclear policy, China has assumed it might have to absorb an initial nuclear blow while ensuring leadership and strategic assets survive.

China determined it needed to update and expand its military UGF program in the mid- to late-1980s. This modernization effort took on a renewed urgency following China's observation of U.S. and NATO air operations during the 1991 Gulf War, as well as air operations during OPERATION ALLIED FORCE in Kosovo in 1999. A new emphasis on "winning high tech battles" in the future precipitated research into advanced tunneling and construction methods. These military campaigns convinced China it needed to build more survivable, deeply buried facilities, resulting in the widespread UGF construction effort detected throughout China for the last decade.

Denial and Deception

In historical and contemporary PLA texts, Chinese military theorists routinely emphasize the importance of secrecy and deception for both the protection of personnel and infrastructure and the concealment of sensitive military activities. In 2012 and 2013, the Chinese press featured the PLA using a variety of denial and deception (D&D) methods, including camouflage, decoys, and satellite avoidance activities during training events to protect PRC forces from enemy surveillance and targeting. Key D&D principles identified in official PLA monographs include:

- Conforming to what the enemy expects and creating false images that correspond to the target's psychological tendencies and expectations;

- Detailed pre-planning, centralized control, and operational integration to ensure strategic coherence at the political, diplomatic, and economic levels;

- Extensive, current, and sophisticated understanding of enemy psychology, predisposition, capabilities (particularly C4ISR), intentions, and location; and

- Operational flexibility, rapid response, and the ability and willingness to employ new D&D techniques and devices.

Contemporary PLA writings also indicate that the Chinese view D&D as a critical enabler of psychological shock and force multiplication effects during a surprise attack, allowing the PLA to offset the advantages of a technologically superior enemy and to reinforce its military superiority against weaker opponents.

Sea-Based Platforms. China continues to produce the JIN-class SSBNs, with three already delivered and as many as two more in varying stages of construction. The JIN-class SSBN will eventually carry the JL-2 SLBM with an estimated range of 7,400 km. Together, these will give the PLA Navy its first credible long-range sea-based nuclear deterrent.

Future Efforts. China is working on a range of technologies to attempt to counter U.S. and other countries' ballistic missile defense systems, including MIRVs, decoys, chaff, jamming, and thermal shielding. China's official media also cites numerous Second Artillery training exercises featuring maneuver, camouflage, and launch operations under simulated combat conditions, which are intended to increase survivability. Together with the increased mobility and survivability of the new generation of missiles, these technologies and training enhancements strengthen China's nuclear force and enhance its strategic strike capabilities. Further increases in the number of mobile ICBMs and the beginning of SSBN deterrence patrols will force the PLA to implement more sophisticated command and control systems and processes that safeguard the integrity of nuclear release authority for a larger, more dispersed force.

Anti-Access/Area Denial (A2/AD). As part of its planning for military contingencies, China continues to develop measures to deter or counter third-party intervention, particularly by the United States. China's approach to dealing with this challenge is manifested in a sustained effort to develop the capability to attack, at long ranges, military forces that might deploy to or operate in the western Pacific, which the Department of Defense characterizes as "anti-access and area denial" (A2/AD) capabilities. China is pursuing a variety of air, sea, undersea, space and counterspace, and information warfare systems and operational concepts to achieve this capability, moving toward an array of overlapping, multilayered offensive capabilities extending from China's coast into the western Pacific.

An essential element, if not a fundamental prerequisite, of China's emerging A2/AD regime is the ability to control and dominate the information spectrum in all dimensions of the modern battlespace. PLA authors often cite the need in modern warfare to control information, sometimes termed "information blockade" or "information dominance," and to seize the initiative and gain an information advantage in the early phases of a campaign to achieve air and sea superiority. China is improving information and operational security to protect its own information structures and is also developing electronic and information warfare capabilities, including denial and deception, to defeat those of its adversaries. China's "information blockade" likely envisions the use of military and non-military instruments of state power across the battlespace, including in cyberspace and outer space to deny information superiority to its adversaries. China's investments in advanced electronic warfare (EW) systems, counterspace weapons, and computer network operations (CNO) – combined with propaganda and denial through opacity – reflect the emphasis and priority China's leaders place on building capability for information advantage.

In more traditional domains, China's A2/AD focus appears oriented toward restricting or controlling access to China's periphery, including the western Pacific. The development of China's conventionally armed missiles has been rapid, even in the context of overall Chinese military modernization. As recently as ten years ago, several hundred short-range ballistic missiles might have ranged targets in Taiwan, but China effectively had no capability to strike many other locations in or beyond the first island chain (such as U.S. bases in Okinawa or Guam). Today, however, China has more than 1,000 conventionally armed ballistic missiles. U.S. bases on Okinawa are in range of a growing number of Chinese MRBMs, and Guam could potentially be reached by air-launched cruise missiles.

Chinese missiles have also become far more accurate and are now better suited to strike regional air bases, logistics facilities, and other ground-based infrastructure, which Chinese military analysts have concluded are vulnerabilities in modern warfare. China is fielding an array of conventionally armed ballistic missiles, ground- and air-launched land-attack cruise missiles, special operations forces, and cyber warfare capabilities to hold such targets at risk throughout the region.

In a near-term conflict, PLA Navy operations would likely begin in the offshore and coastal areas with attacks by coastal defense cruise missiles, maritime strike aircraft, and smaller combatants and extend as far as the second island chain and Strait of Malacca using large surface ships and submarines. As the PLA Navy gains experience and acquires larger numbers of more capable platforms, including those with long-range air defense, it will expand the depth of these operations further into the western Pacific. The PLA Navy may also develop a new capability for ship-based land-attack using cruise missiles. China views long-range anti-ship cruise missiles as a key weapon in this type of operation and is developing multiple advanced types and the platforms to employ them for this purpose. These platforms include conventional and nuclear-powered attack submarines (KILO SS, SONG SS, YUAN SSP, SHANG SSN), surface combatants (LUYANG III DDG [Type 052D], LUZHOU DDG [Type 051C], LUYANG I/II DDG [Type 052B/C], SOVREMENNY II-class DDG, JIANGKAI II FFG [Type 054A], JIANGDAO FFL [Type 056]), and maritime strike aircraft (FB-7A, H-6G and the Su-30MK2).

China would face several shortcomings in a near-term conflict, however. First, the PLA's

31

deep-water anti-submarine warfare capability seems to lag behind its air and surface warfare capabilities. Second, it is not clear whether China has the capability to collect accurate targeting information and pass it to launch platforms in time for successful strikes against targets at sea beyond the first island chain. Chinese submarines do, however, already possess some capability to hold surface ships at risk, and China is working to overcome shortcomings in other areas.

Counterspace. PLA strategists regard the ability to use space-based systems – and to deny adversaries access to space-based systems – as central to enabling modern, "informationized" warfare. Although PLA doctrine does not appear to address space operations as a unique operational "campaign," space operations form an integral component of other PLA campaigns and would serve a key role in enabling A2/AD operations. A PLA analysis of U.S. and coalition military operations reinforced the importance of operations in space to enable "informationized" warfare, claiming that "space is the commanding point for the information battlefield." PLA writings emphasize the necessity of "destroying, damaging, and interfering with the enemy's reconnaissance ... and communications satellites," suggesting that such systems, as well as navigation and early warning satellites, could be among the targets of attacks designed to "blind and deafen the enemy." The same PLA analysis of U.S. and coalition military operations also states that "destroying or capturing satellites and other sensors ... will deprive an opponent of initiative on the battlefield and [make it difficult] for them to bring their precision guided weapons into full play.""

The PLA is acquiring a range of technologies to improve China's space and counterspace capabilities. In addition to directed energy weapons and satellite jammers, China demonstrated a direct-ascent kinetic kill capability against satellites in low Earth orbit when it destroyed the defunct Chinese FY-1C weather satellite during a test in January 2007.

Building an Informationized Military. Chinese military writings describe informationized warfare as an asymmetric form of warfare used to defeat a technologically superior, information-dependent adversary through dominance of the battlefield's information space. Information operations encompass defensive and offensive military actions and focus on defending PLA information systems, while disrupting or destroying an adversary's information systems. Chinese writings view informationized warfare as a way to weaken an adversary's ability to acquire, transmit, process, and use information during war and discuss it as a way to force an adversary to capitulate before the onset of conflict. The PLA conducts military exercises simulating operations in complex electromagnetic environments and likely views conventional and cyber operations as a means of achieving information dominance. The PLA GSD

Fourth Department (Electronic Countermeasures and Radar) would likely use jamming and electronic warfare, cyberspace operations, and deception to augment counterspace and other kinetic operations during a wartime scenario to deny an adversary's use of information systems. "Simultaneous and parallel" operations would involve strikes against U.S. warships, aircraft, and associated supply craft, as well as the use of information attacks to hamper tactical and operational communications and computer networks. These operations could have a significant effect upon an adversary's navigational and targeting radars.

Air and Air Defense. China's A2/AD capabilities will be bolstered by the development of fifth-generation fighter aircraft, which is not likely to be fielded before 2018. Key characteristics of fifth-generation fighters include high maneuverability, low observability, and an internal weapons bay. Other key features include modern avionics and sensors that offer more timely situational awareness for operations in network-centric combat environments, radars with advanced targeting capabilities and protection against enemy electronic countermeasures, and integrated electronic warfare systems with advanced communication and GPS navigation functions. These next-generation aircraft will improve China's existing fleet of fourth-generation aircraft (Russian-built Su-27/Su-30 and indigenous J-10 and J-11B fighters) to

support regional air superiority and strike operations. Additionally, China's continuing upgrades to its bomber fleet gives the bombers the capability to carry long-range cruise missiles. Similarly, the acquisition and development of longer-range UAVs will increase China's ability to conduct long-range reconnaissance and strike operations.

China is incrementally advancing its development and employment of UAVs. According to a 2013 report by the Defense Science Board, China's move into unmanned systems is "alarming" and combines unlimited resources with technological awareness that might allow China to match or even outpace U.S. spending on unmanned systems in the future. During September 2013, a probable Chinese UAV was noted for the first time conducting reconnaissance over the East China Sea. This past year, China unveiled details of four UAVs under development, three of which are designed to carry weapons: the Xianglong (Soaring Dragon); Yilong (Pterodactyl); Sky Saber; and Lijian, China's first stealthy flying wing UAV, for which China announced its first maiden flight on November 21, 2013.

China's ground-based air defense will likely be focused on countering long-range airborne strike platforms with increasing numbers of advanced SAMs. These include the indigenous CSA-9 (HQ-9) and Russian SA-10 (S-300PMU) and SA-20 (S-300PMU1/PMU2), which have the advertised capability to protect against both aircraft and low-flying cruise missiles. China continues to pursue acquisition of the Russian extremely long-range SA-X-21b (S-400) SAM system (400 km)' and is also expected to continue research and development to extend the range of the domestic CSA-9 SAM to beyond 200 km.

In conjunction with procuring more capable military equipment, China is also increasing the complexity of air and air defense training. During late September and October 2013, the PLA conducted MISSION ACTION 2013C, the third and final phase of the overall MISSION ACTION 2013 exercise. The focus of this third phase was as a large-scale, long-range joint assault involving nearly 100 bomber, fighter, and special mission aircraft, and more than 10,000 personnel.

Following on the heels of MISSION ACTION 2013C, also during September and October 2013, China engaged in a complex long-distance maritime exercise. Naval units from all three fleets of the PLA Navy participated in the western Pacific exercise. Not only was the size and location of this exercise noteworthy, but it was described by PLA Navy RADM Liao Shining, Executive Deputy Commander of the MANEUVER-5 exercise (also referred to as JIDONG- 5 and MOBILITY -5), as the first of its size carried out with no scripts.

Ballistic Missile Defense. China is pursuing ballistic missile defense capabilities in order to provide further protection of China's mainland and strategic assets. China's existing long-range SAM inventory offers limited capability against ballistic missiles. The SA-20 PMU2, the most advanced SAM Russia offers for export, has the advertised capability to engage ballistic missiles with ranges of 1,000 km and speeds of 2,800 meters per second (m/s). China's domestic CSA-9 long-range SAM system is expected to have a limited capability to provide point defense against tactical ballistic missiles with ranges up to 500 km. China is pursuing research and development of a missile defense umbrella consisting of kinetic energy intercepts at exo-atmospheric altitudes (>80 km), as well as intercepts of ballistic missiles and other aerospace vehicles within the upper atmosphere. In January 2010, China successfully intercepted a ballistic missile at mid-course using a ground-based missile.

Cyber Activities Directed against the U.S. Department of Defense. In 2013, numerous computer systems around the world, including those owned by the U.S. Government, continued to be targeted for intrusions, some of which appear to be attributable directly to the Chinese government and military. These intrusions were focused on exfiltrating information. China is using its computer network exploitation (CNE) capability to support intelligence collection against the U.S. diplomatic, economic, and defense industrial base sectors that support U.S. national defense programs. The information targeted could potentially be used to benefit China's defense industry, high-technology industries, policymakers' interest in U.S. leadership thinking on key China issues, and military planners' understanding of U.S. defense networks, logistics, and related military capabilities that could be exploited during a crisis. The accesses and skills required for these intrusions are similar to those necessary to conduct computer network attacks.

Cyber Warfare in China's Military. China's 2010 Defense White Paper noted China's own concern over foreign cyber warfare efforts and highlighted the importance of cybersecurity in China's national defense. Cyber warfare could support Chinese military operations in three key areas. First, it will enable data collection for intelligence and computer network attack. Second, it constrains an adversary's actions or slows their response. Third, it is as a force multiplier when coupled with kinetic attacks.

Developing cyber capabilities for warfare is consistent with authoritative PLA military writings. Two military doctrinal writings, *Science of Strategy*, and *Science of Campaigns*, identify information warfare (IW) as integral to achieving information superiority and an effective means for countering a stronger foe. Although neither document identifies the specific criteria for employing computer network attack against an adversary, both advocate developing capabilities to compete in this medium.

The Science of Strategy and *Science of Campaigns* detail the effectiveness of IW and CNO in conflicts and advocate targeting adversary C2 and logistics networks to affect their ability to operate during the early stages of conflict. As *Science of Strategy* explains, "In the information war, the command and control system is the heart of information collection, control, and application on the battlefield. It is also the nerve center of the entire battlefield."

Role of Electronic Warfare in Future Conflict

The PLA believes electronic warfare (EW) is one method to reduce or eliminate U.S. technological advantage. Chinese EW doctrine emphasizes using electromagnetic spectrum weapons to suppress or deceive enemy electronic equipment. PLA EW strategy focuses on radio, radar, optical, infrared, and microwave frequencies, in addition to computer and information systems.

Chinese strategy stresses that EW is a vital fourth dimension to combat and should be considered equal to ground, sea, and air, and that it can be decisive during military operations. The Chinese see EW as an important force multiplier and would likely employ it in support of all combat arms and services during a conflict.

PLA EW units have conducted jamming and anti-jamming operations, testing the military's understanding of EW weapons, equipment, and performance, which helped improve confidence in conducting force-on-force, real-equipment confrontation operations in simulated EW environments. The advances in research and deployment of EW weapons are being tested in these exercises and have proven effective. These EW weapons include jamming equipment against multiple communication and radar systems and GPS. EW systems are also being deployed with other sea and air-based platforms intended for both offensive and defensive operations.

Systems and Capabilities Enabling Power Projection. China has prioritized land-based ballistic and cruise missile programs to extend its strike warfare capabilities further from its borders. It is developing and testing several new classes and variants of offensive missiles, forming additional missile units, upgrading older missile systems, and developing methods to counter ballistic missile defenses. The Second Artillery has deployed more than 1,000 SRBMs to garrisons across from Taiwan and is fielding cruise missiles, including the ground-launched CJ-10 LACM. China continues to field an ASBM based on a variant of the CSS-5 (DF-21) MRBM that it began deploying in 2010. This missile provides the PLA the capability to attack large ships, including aircraft carriers, in the western Pacific. The CSS-5 Mod 5 has a range exceeding 1,500 km and is armed with a maneuverable warhead.

The PLA Navy continues the development and deployment of ship-, submarine-, and aircraft-deployed ASCMs – a mix of Russian- and Chinese-built missiles – which extend China's strike range. Additionally, China may develop the capability to arm the new LUYANG Class-III DDG with LACMs, giving the PLA Navy its first land attack capability. In late October, Japan observed Chinese H-6 bombers and Y-8 reconnaissance aircraft flying over the Miyako Strait to the western Pacific Ocean. The PLA Navy Air Force continues to make incremental improvements in its air power projection capabilities.

The PLA Air Force is continuing to improve its ability to conduct offensive and defensive offshore operations such as strike, air and missile defense, strategic mobility, and early warning and reconnaissance missions. China is developing stealth aircraft technology, with a second stealth fighter, designated the J-31, which conducted its maiden flight on October 31, 2012, following on the heels of the J-20. To address its strategic airlift deficiency, China is also testing a new heavy-lift transport aircraft, probably identified as the Y-20. This aircraft began flight testing in January 2013. In addition to being China's first indigenous heavy-lift jet transport, the Y-20 could also acquire additional missions such as an airborne warning and control system (AWACS) and as an aerial refueling tanker.

With refurbishment of the Soviet KUZNETSOV-class aircraft carrier completed in 2012, China has named the vessel CV-16, LIAONING, and now has an initial means to conduct carrier operations. During 2013, China focused on integrating the LIAONING with its J-15 aircraft as well as working out other carrier operations. Although the LIAONING is serving in what officials describe as an "experimental" capacity, they also indicate that China will build additional carriers possessing more capability than the ski-jump-configured LIAONING. Such a carrier force would be capable of improved endurance and of carrying and launching more varied types of aircraft, including electronic warfare, early warning, and anti-submarine, to increase the potential striking power of a Chinese "battle group" in safeguarding China's interests in areas outside China's immediate periphery. The carriers would most likely perform such missions as patrolling economically important sea lanes and conducting naval diplomacy, regional deterrence, and humanitarian assistance/disaster relief.

Capabilities to Realize a "Blue Water" Navy. The PLA Navy remains at the forefront of China's military efforts to extend its operational reach beyond the western Pacific and into what China calls the "far seas." Missions in these areas include: protecting important sea lanes from terrorism, maritime piracy, and foreign interdiction; providing humanitarian assistance/disaster relief; conducting naval diplomacy and regional deterrence; and training to prevent a third party, such as the United States, from interfering with operations off China's coast in a Taiwan, East China Sea, or South China Sea conflict. The PLA Navy's ability to perform these missions is modest but growing as it gains more experience operating in distant waters and acquires larger and more advanced platforms. The PLA Navy's goal over the coming decades is to become a stronger regional force that is able to project power across the greater Asia-Pacific region for long-term, high-intensity operations. However, logistics and intelligence support

remain key obstacles, particularly in the Indian Ocean.

In the last several years, the PLA Navy's distant seas experience has derived primarily from counterpiracy missions in the Gulf of Aden and long-distance task group deployments beyond the first island chain in the western Pacific. China continues to sustain a three-ship presence in the Gulf of Aden to protect Chinese merchant shipping from maritime piracy. This operation is China's first enduring naval operation beyond the Asia region.

Additionally, the PLA Navy continues to conduct military activities within its nine-dash line and the claimed exclusive economic zones (EEZs) of other nations, without the permission of those coastal states. For example, in March 2013, sailors aboard a group of surface combatants reportedly performed an oath-taking ceremony at James Shoal. The United States considers military activities in foreign EEZs to be lawful and notes that similar PLA Navy activity in foreign EEZs undercuts China's decades-old position that such activities in China's EEZ are unlawful.

The PLA Navy has made long-distance deployments a routine part of the annual training cycle. In 2013, it deployed task groups beyond the first island chain nine times with formations as large as eight ships. These deployments included a three-ship surface action group deployment to South America, the first-ever such deployment. Deployments such as these are designed to complete a number of training requirements, including long-distance navigation, C2, and multi-discipline warfare in deep sea environments beyond the range of land-based air defense.

The PLA Navy's force structure continues to evolve, incorporating more platforms with the versatility for both offshore and long-distance operations. China is engaged in series production of the LUYANG III-class DDG, the JIANGKAI II-class FFG, and the JIANGDAO-class FFL. China might begin construction on a new Type 081-class amphibious assault ship within the next five years. China will probably build multiple aircraft carriers over the next 15 years.

Limited logistical support remains a key obstacle preventing the PLA Navy from operating more extensively beyond East Asia, particularly in the Indian Ocean. China desires to expand its access to logistics in the Indian Ocean and will likely establish several access points in this area in the next 10 years. These arrangements likely will take the form of agreements for refueling, replenishment, crew rest, and low-level maintenance.

China's Approach to Maritime Security

During the 2012 Scarborough Reef and 2013 Senkaku Islands tensions, the China Maritime Surveillance (CMS) and Fisheries Law Enforcement Command (FLEC) ships were responsible for directly asserting Chinese sovereignty on a daily basis, while the PLA Navy maintained a more distant presence from the immediate vicinity of the contested waters. China prefers to use its civilian maritime agencies around these islands, and uses the PLA Navy in a back-up role or as an escalatory measure. China's diplomats also apply pressure on rival claimants. China identifies its territorial sovereignty as a core interest and emphasizes its willingness to protect against actions that China perceives challenge Chinese sovereignty. China almost certainly wants to assert its maritime dominance without triggering too harsh of a regional backlash.

In 2013, China consolidated four of its maritime law enforcement agencies into the China Coast Guard (CCG). Subordinate to the Ministry of Public Security, the CCG is responsible for a wide range of missions, including maritime sovereignty enforcement missions, anti-smuggling, maritime rescue and salvage, protecting fisheries resources, and general law enforcement. Prior to the consolidation, different agencies were responsible for each of these mission sets, creating organizational redundancies and complicating interagency coordination.

In the next decade, a new force of civilian maritime ships will afford China the capability to patrol its territorial claims more robustly in the East China and the South China Seas. China is continuing with the second half of a modernization and construction program for the CCG. The first half of this program, from 2004 to 2008, resulted in the addition of almost 20 ocean-going patrol ships. The second half of this program, from 2011 to 2015, includes at least 30 new ships for the CCG. Several less capable patrol ships will be decommissioned during this period. In addition, the CCG will likely build more than 100 new patrol craft and smaller units, both to increase capability and to replace old units. Overall, The CCG's total force level is expected to increase by 25 percent. Some of these ships will have the capability to embark helicopters, a capability that only a few MLE ships currently have. The enlargement and modernization of China's MLE forces will improve China's ability to enforce its maritime sovereignty.

Military Operations Other Than War. China's military continues to emphasize Military Operations Other Than War (MOOTW) including emergency response, counterterrorism, international rescue, disaster relief, peacekeeping, and other security tasks. China's 2010 Defense White Paper cited the use of its military for these purposes as a means of maintaining social harmony and stability. These missions support the "New Historic Missions" while giving the PLA opportunities to acquire operational and mobilization proficiency in addition to strengthening civil-military relations.

In 2013 the PLA Navy deployed for the third time the hospital ship ANWEI on a four-month deployment to South and Southeast Asia. HARMONIOUS MISSION 2013 conducted medical port calls in Brunei, Maldives, Pakistan, India, Bangladesh, Burma, Indonesia, and Cambodia. China also deployed the ANWEI to the Philippines in November 2013 following Typhoon Haiyan in the first operational deployment of the ship. Additionally, the PLA continues to support UN peacekeeping operations and participate in military exercises as a member of the Shanghai Cooperation Organization (SCO).

Precision Strike

Short-Range Ballistic Missiles (< 1,000 km): The Second Artillery had more than 1,000 SRBMs at the end of 2013. The Second Artillery continues to field advanced variants with improved ranges and accuracy in addition to more sophisticated payloads, while gradually replacing earlier generations that do not possess true precision strike capability.

Medium-Range Ballistic Missiles (1,000-3,000 km): The PLA is fielding conventional MRBMs to increase the range at which it can conduct precision strikes against land targets and naval ships (including aircraft carriers) operating far from China's shores out to the first island chain.

Intermediate-Range Ballistic Missiles (3,000-5,000 km): The PLA is developing conventional IRBMs that increase its capability for near-precision strike out to the second island chain. The PLA Navy also is improving its over-the-horizon (OTH) targeting capability with sky wave and surface wave OTH radars, which can be used in conjunction with reconnaissance satellites to locate targets at great distances from China (thereby supporting long-range precision strikes, including employment of ASBMs).

Land-Attack Cruise Missiles: The PLA continues to field air- and ground-launched LACMs for stand-off, precision strikes. Air-launched cruise missiles include the YJ-63, KD-88, and the CJ-20. China recently revealed the CM-802AKG LACM.

Ground Attack Munitions: The PLA Air Force has a small number of tactical air-to-surface missiles (ASMs) as well as precision-guided munitions including all-weather, satellite-guided bombs, anti-radiation missiles and laser-guided bombs. China is developing smaller-sized ASMs such as the AR-1, HJ-10 anti-tank, Blue Arrow 7 laser-guided and KD-2 in conjunction with its increasing development of UAVs. China is also adapting GPS-guided munitions such as the FT-5 and LS-6 that are similar to the U.S. Joint Direct Attack Munitions (JDAM) to UAVs.

Anti-Ship Cruise Missiles: The PLA Navy deploys the domestically produced ship-launched YJ-62 ASCM; the Russian SS-N-22/SUNBURN supersonic ASCM, which is fitted on China's SOVREMENNY-class DDGs acquired from Russia; and the Russian SS-N-27B/SIZZLER supersonic ASCM on China's Russian-built KILO SS. It has, or is acquiring, nearly a dozen ASCM variants, ranging from the 1950s-era CSS-N-2 to the modern Russian-made SS-N-22 and SS-N-27B. The pace of ASCM research, development, and production has accelerated over the past decade. In addition, the PLA Navy Air Force employs the YJ-83K ASCM on its JH-7 and H-6G aircraft. China has also developed the YJ-12 ASCM for the Navy. The new missile provides an increased threat to naval assets, due to its long range and supersonic speeds. It is capable of being launched from H-6 bombers.

Anti-Radiation Weapons: China is starting to integrate an indigenous version of the Russian Kh-31P (AS-17) known as the YJ-91 into its fighter-bomber force. The PLA imported Israeli-made HARPY UAVs and Russian-made anti-radiation missiles during the 1990s.

Artillery-Delivered High-Precision Munitions: The PLA is developing or deploying artillery systems with the range to strike targets within or even across the Taiwan Strait, including the PHL-03 300 mm multiple-rocket launcher (MRL) (100+ km range) and the longer-range AR-3 dual-caliber MRL (out to 220 km).

China's Internal Security Forces

China's internal security forces primarily consist of the People's Armed Police (PAP), the Ministry of Public Security (MPS), and the PLA. The PAP is a paramilitary organization whose primary mission is domestic security. It falls under the dual command of the CMC and the State Council. Although there are different types of PAP units, such as border security and firefighting, the largest is internal security. PAP units are organized into "contingents" in each province, autonomous region, and centrally administered city. In addition, 14 PLA divisions were transferred to the PAP in the mid- to late- 1990s to form "mobile divisions" that can deploy outside their home province. The official budget for China's internal security forces exceeds that of the PLA.

The key mission of the MPS is domestic law enforcement and the "maintenance of social security and order" with duties including anti-rioting and anti-terrorism. There are about 1.9 million MPS police officers spread throughout local public security bureaus across the country.

The PLA's principal focus is on preserving the continued rule of the Chinese Communist Party. As such, the PLA may be used for internal or external stability missions as needed. For example, the PLA may provide transportation, logistics, and intelligence. China may also task the military to assist local public security forces with internal security roles, including protection of infrastructure and maintaining public order.

Chinese leaders perceive threats to the country's internal security coming from popular protests regarding social, economic, environmental, and political problems. China also perceives a security challenge from external non-state actors, such as the separatist East Turkestan Islamic Movement and its alleged connection with ethnic Uighur nationalist movements in the Xinjiang region.

In 2013, China continued to follow the pattern of using security forces to quell incidents ranging from anti-foreign sentiment to socio-economic protests. PAP units, particularly the mobile security divisions, also continued to receive extensive equipment upgrades. China activated security forces several times in 2013 in response to incidents of violence and also in preparation of sensitive anniversaries such as the July 5 anniversary of the 2009 Uyghur riots in Urumqi. In April, China dispatched more than 1,000 paramilitary police to Xinjiang after riots resulted in the death of 21 people. Later in June, at least 1,000 paramilitary police shut down large sections of Urumqi and conducted 24-hour patrols in military vehicles after clashes left 35 people dead. In October, paramilitary police were deployed to Biru County in the Tibet Autonomous Region to crack down on Tibetans who protested an order to fly the Chinese national flag at home.

4

RESOURCES FOR FORCE MODERNIZATION

OVERVIEW

The PLA continues to decrease its reliance on foreign weapon acquisitions as China's defense-industrial and research bases mature. However, the PLA still looks to foreign assistance to fill some critical near-term capability gaps. China continues to leverage foreign investments, commercial joint ventures, academic exchanges, the experience of repatriated Chinese students and researchers, and state-sponsored industrial and technical espionage to increase the level of technologies and expertise available to support military research, development, and acquisition. China's long-term goal is to create a wholly indigenous defense industrial sector, augmented by a strong commercial sector, to meet the needs of PLA modernization and to compete as a top-tier supplier in the global arms market. China draws from diverse sources to support PLA modernization, including: domestic defense investments, indigenous defense industrial development, a growing research and development/science and technology base, dual-use technologies, and foreign technology acquisition.

MILITARY EXPENDITURES TRENDS

On March 5, 2013, China announced a 5.7 percent increase in its annual military budget to $119.5 billion USD, continuing more than two decades of sustained annual defense spending increases. Analysis of data from 2004 through 2013 indicates China's officially disclosed military budget grew at an average of 9.4 percent per year in inflation-adjusted terms over the period. China has the fiscal strength and political will to support defense spending growth at comparable levels for the foreseeable future. Continued increases will support PLA modernization efforts and facilitate China's move toward a more professional force.

Estimating China's Actual Military Expenditures. Using 2013 prices and exchange rates, the Department of Defense (DoD) estimates that China's total military-related spending for 2013 exceeds $145 billion. However, it is difficult to estimate actual PLA military expenses due to China's poor accounting transparency and incomplete transition from a command economy. China's published military budget omits several major categories of expenditure, such as procurement of foreign weapons and equipment.

2013 Defense Budget Comparison (Adjusted for Inflation)	
	Billion (USD)
China (Official Budget)	$119.5
Russia (National Defense Budget)	$69.5
Japan	$56.9
India	$39.2
Republic of Korea	$31.0
Taiwan	$10.8

Comparison of China's official defense budget with those of other regional powers

DEVELOPMENTS AND TRENDS IN CHINA'S DEFENSE INDUSTRY

Defense Sector Reform. China's defense industry has undergone a dramatic transformation since the late-1990s, and its companies and research institutes continue to re-organize in an effort to improve weapon system research, development and production capabilities. China also continues to improve business practices, streamline bureaucracy, shorten developmental timelines, and improve quality control.

In 1998, China adopted a comprehensive strategy for improving defense industrial capabilities. This strategy called for selective modernization in key capabilities areas, increased civil-military industrial integration to leverage available dual-use technologies, and the acquisition of advanced foreign weapons, materiel, and technologies. An overarching goal of these reforms was to introduce the "Four Mechanisms" of competition, evaluation, supervision, and encouragement into the entire defense industrial system. In 1999, the State Council implemented structural reforms within defense industries to increase competition and efficiency and to make China's defense industry more responsive to the PLA's operational requirements. Each of China's five state-owned defense conglomerates was split into two enterprises, creating a parallel structure in which each would produce both defense and civilian products, encouraging the potential for competition. The production of civilian-use commercial products allows legitimate access to the latest industry and dual-use technologies, which can then be used to support military production. Commercial operations also provide revenue streams to support defense-related activities.

In 2003, the Sixteenth Party Congress introduced the concept of locating military potential in civilian capabilities. It called for building a civilian industrial sector capable of meeting the needs of military force modernization. In a further move to strengthen the defense sector and improve oversight, China created a new super-ministry in 2008. The Ministry of Industry and Informationization (MIIT) was charged with facilitating civil-military integration and the coordinated development of advanced technology and industry. Other structural reforms were adopted to strengthen defense research, development, and production and to bring them more in line with market principles.

China is also emphasizing integration of defense and civilian sectors to leverage output from China's expanding science and technology base. Select defense firms operate research institutes with academic departments, some of which are capable of granting advanced degrees. These institutes serve to focus scientific research on cutting-edge military technologies and to groom the next generation of scientists and engineers who will support defense research, development, and production. These institutes also provide an access point to international resources and scientific research networks. Chinese practitioners and students at these defense institutes regularly attend conferences, present research findings, and publish scholarly articles.

The China Academy of Sciences (CAS) also plays a key role in facilitating research that supports advancements in military modernization. The CAS Institute of Mechanics is one example, with a focus on scientific innovation and high-tech integration in aerospace technology, environmental engineering, and energy resources. Specific areas of emphasis include nano-scale and micro-scale mechanics, high temperature gas and supersonic flight technologies, and advanced manufacturing. In May 2012, the Institute announced successful acceptance testing of its new super-large JF12 hypersonic wind tunnel, reportedly the largest in the world, capable of replicating flying conditions at mach 5 to 9. This project was one of eight detailed in China's National Mid- and Long-Term Scientific and Technological Development Outline Plan (2006-2020). This facility and others like it sponsored by CAS will support research and development efforts in China's civilian and military aerospace sector.

MILITARY EQUIPMENT MODERNIZATION TRENDS

China's defense industry resource and investment prioritization and allocation favors missile and space systems, followed by maritime assets and aircraft, and lastly, ground force materiel. China is developing and producing increasingly advanced systems, augmented through selected investments into foreign designs and reverse engineering. China's defense industries are increasing the quality of output in all of these areas as well as increasing overall production capacities. Over the past decade, China has made dramatic improvements in all defense industrial production sectors and, in some areas, is comparable to other major weapon system producers like Russia and the European Union.

Missile and Space Industry. China's production of a range of ballistic, cruise, air-to-air, and surface-to-air missiles for the PLA and for export has likely been enhanced by upgrades to primary final assembly and rocket motor production facilities over the past few years. China's space launch vehicle industry is expanding to support satellite launch services and the manned space program. The majority of China's missile programs, including its ballistic and cruise missile systems, is comparable to other international top-tier producers, while its surface-to-air missile systems lag behind global leaders. China's missile industry modernization efforts have positioned it well for the foreseeable future.

Naval and Shipbuilding Industry. Shipyard expansion and modernization have increased China's shipbuilding capacity and capability, generating benefits for all types of military projects, including submarines, surface combatants, naval aviation, and sealift assets. Collaboration between China's two largest state-owned shipbuilders, China State Shipbuilding Corporation (CSSC) and China Shipbuilding Industry Corporation (CSIC), in shared ship designs and construction information will likely increase shipbuilding efficiency. China continues to invest in foreign suppliers for some propulsion units, but is becoming increasingly self-reliant. China is among the top ship-producing nations in the world and is currently pursuing an indigenous aircraft carrier program. To date, China has not produced a non-carrier surface combatant larger than a destroyer, but is outfitting these ships with increasingly sophisticated anti-surface, -air, and -subsurface defensive and offensive capabilities. China is using more sophisticated ship design and construction program management techniques and software.

Armaments Industry. There have been production capacity advances in almost every area of PLA ground forces systems, including production of new tanks, armored personnel carriers, air defense artillery systems and artillery pieces. However, China still relies on foreign acquisition to fill gaps in select critical technical capabilities, such as turbine aircraft engines. China is capable of producing ground weapon systems at or near world standards, though quality deficiencies persist with some export equipment.

Aviation Industry. China's commercial and military aviation industries have advanced to produce indigenously improved versions of older aircraft and modern fourth- and fifth-generation fighters, which incorporate low-observable technologies, as well as attack helicopters. China's commercial aircraft industry has invested in high-precision and technologically advanced machine tools, avionics, and other components that can also be used in the production of military aircraft. However, production in the aircraft industry will be limited by its reliance on foreign sourcing for dependable, proven aircraft engines. Infrastructure and experience for the production of large-body commercial and military aircraft are believed to be limited, but growing with continued investments.

Foreign Technology Acquisition. Key areas where China continues to supplement indigenous military modernization efforts through targeted foreign technologies include engines for aircraft and tanks, solid state electronics and microprocessors, guidance and control systems, and enabling technologies such as cutting-edge precision machine tools, advanced diagnostic and forensic equipment, and computer-assisted design, manufacturing, and engineering. China often pursues these foreign technologies for the purpose of reverse engineering or to supplement indigenous military modernization efforts.

China seeks some high-tech components and certain major end items, particularly from Russia, that it has difficulty producing domestically. China is pursuing advanced Russian defense equipment such as the SA-X-21b (S-400) surface-to-air missile system, Su-35 fighter aircraft, and a new joint-design and production program for diesel-electric submarines based on the Russian PETERSBURG/LADA-class. Between 2011 and 2012, Russia agreed to sell China IL-76 transport aircraft and Mi-171 helicopters. Russia's concerns about intellectual property protections affect the types and quantities of advanced arms or associated production technologies it is willing to transfer to China. China also has signed significant purchase contracts with Ukraine in recent years, including contracts for assault hovercraft and aircraft engines.

Science and Technology Development Goals through 2020. China's *National Medium- and Long-Term Program for Science and Technology Development* (2006-2020), issued by the State Council in February 2006, seeks to transform China into an "innovation-oriented society by 2020." The plan defines China's science and technology focus in terms of "basic research," "leading-edge technologies," "key fields and priority subjects," and "major special items," all of which have military applications.

Basic Research. As part of a broad effort to expand basic research capabilities, China identified five areas that have military applications as major strategic needs or science research plans requiring active government involvement and funding:

> Material design and preparation;

> Manufacturing in extreme environmental conditions;

> Aeronautic and astronautic mechanics;

> Information technology development; and,

> Nanotechnology research.

In nanotechnology, China has progressed from virtually no research or funding in 2002 to being a close second to the United States in total government investment.

Leading-Edge Technologies. China is focusing on the following technologies for rapid development:

> Information Technology: Priorities include intelligent perception technologies, *ad hoc* networks, and virtual-reality technologies;

> New Materials: Priorities include smart materials and structures, high-temperature superconducting technologies, and highly efficient energy materials technologies;

> Advanced Manufacturing: Priorities include extreme manufacturing technologies and intelligent service advanced machine tools;

> Advanced Energy Technologies: Priorities include hydrogen energy and fuel cell technologies, alternative fuels, and advanced vehicle technologies;

> Marine Technologies: Priorities include three-dimensional maritime environmental monitoring technologies, fast, multi-parameter ocean floor survey technologies, and deep-sea operations technologies; and,

> Laser and Aerospace Technologies: Priorities include development of chemical and solid laser state technologies to field a weapon-grade system ultimately from ground-based and airborne platforms.

Key Fields and Priority Subjects. China has identified certain industries and technology groups with potential to provide technological breakthroughs, remove technical obstacles across industries, and improve international competitiveness. Specifically, China's defense industries are pursuing advanced manufacturing, information technology, and defense technologies. Examples include radar, counterspace capabilities, secure C4ISR, smart materials, and low-observable technologies.

Major Special Items. China has also identified 16 "major special items" for which it plans to develop or expand indigenous capabilities. These include core electronic components, high-end universal chips and operating system software, very large-scale integrated circuit manufacturing, next-generation broadband wireless mobile communications, high-grade numerically controlled machine tools, large aircraft, high-resolution satellites, and lunar exploration.

Espionage Activities Supporting China's Military Modernization. China uses a large, well-organized network of enterprises, defense factories, affiliated research institutes, and computer network operations to facilitate the collection of sensitive information, export-controlled technologies, and basic research and science supporting U.S. defense system modernization. Many of the organizations making up China's military-industrial complex have both military and civilian research and development functions. This network of government-affiliated companies and research institutes often enables the PLA to either access, transfer, or purchase sensitive and dual-use technologies or maintain contact with knowledgeable U.S. and foreign experts under the guise of civilian research and development. Chinese defense enterprises and research institutes target technology conferences and symposia, legitimate contracts and joint commercial ventures, partnerships with foreign firms, and joint development projects to obtain specific technologies or military capabilities.

China also uses its intelligence services and employs other illicit approaches that violate U.S. laws and export controls to obtain key national security technologies, controlled equipment, and other materials not readily obtainable through commercial means or academia.

> In October 2012, Chinese national Lu Futian received 15 months in prison after pleading guilty to export control violations.

Lu's company, Fushine Technology, Inc., shipped a restricted microwave amplifier to Chinese recipient Everjet Science and Technology Corporation without an export license despite notification of the requirement by the U.S. supplier.

> In December 2012, federal prosecutors indicted Chinese nationals Yuan Wanli and Song Jiang for export-control and money laundering violations in connection with a scheme to obtain U.S. dual-use programmable logic devices tested to military specifications. While operating from China, Yuan used a fake website and e-mail addresses created using the name of a legitimate New York-based company to conceal his identity and mislead U.S. suppliers. Yuan is associated with China Wingwish Group Co., Ltd., a China-based company involved in the procurement of dual-use technology.

> In March 2013, Chinese national Liu Sixing received 70 months in prison for lying to Federal agents, transporting stolen property, and violating the Arms Export Control Act, the International Traffic in Arms Regulations, and the Economic Espionage Act. Despite his training in U.S. export control laws, Liu stole thousands of files from his U.S. employer in 2010 detailing the performance and design of guidance systems for missiles, rockets, target locators, and unmanned aerial vehicles and transported them to China. While there, Liu delivered presentations

describing the technology at several Chinese universities, the Chinese Academy of Sciences, and conferences organized by Chinese government entities.

> In May 2013, Chinese national Ma Lisong pled guilty to violating the International Emergency Economic Powers Act after attempting to export weapon-grade carbon fiber to China. Based in China and using an alias, Ma e-mailed a U.S. undercover agent in February 2013 and negotiated the purchase of five tons of export-controlled carbon fiber. Authorities arrested Ma in the United States after he attempted to ship a sample he requested back to China.

> In August 2013, Chinese national Zhang Mingsuan pled guilty to violating the International Emergency Economic Powers Act by attempting to export thousands of pounds of high-grade carbon fiber for use by the Chinese military. During a recorded conversation in 2012, Zhang claimed he urgently needed the fiber in connection with a scheduled test flight of a Chinese fighter plane.

In addition, multiple cases identified since 2009 involved non-ethnic Chinese U.S. citizens and naturalized Chinese U.S. citizens or permanent resident aliens procuring and exporting export controlled items to China. These efforts included attempts to procure and export radiation-hardened programmable semiconductors and computer circuits used in satellites, restricted microwave amplifiers used in weapon guidance systems and communications or radar equipment, high-grade carbon fiber, export-restricted technical data, and thermal imaging cameras.

China's Arms Exports

From 2008 to 2012, China signed approximately $10 billion in agreements for conventional arms worldwide. In 2013 and the coming years, China's arms exports will likely increase modestly as China's domestic defense industry improves. Chinese defense firms are marketing and selling arms worldwide, with the bulk of their sales to Asia, the Middle East, and North Africa. In 2012, China unveiled the Yilong tactical UAV, which will probably be marketed to developing countries.

> Pakistan remains China's primary customer for conventional weapons. China engages in both arms sales and defense industrial cooperation with Islamabad, including co-production of the JF-17 fighter aircraft, F-22P frigates with helicopters, K-8 jet trainers, F-7 fighter aircraft, early warning and control aircraft, tanks, air-to-air missiles, anti-ship cruise missiles, and cooperation on main battle tank production.

> Sub-Saharan African and developing Latin American countries view China as a provider of low-cost weapons with fewer political strings attached compared to other international arms suppliers. China uses arms sales as part of a multifaceted approach to promote trade, secure access to natural resources, and extend its influence in the region.

5

FORCE MODERNIZATION
FOR A TAIWAN CONTINGENCY

OVERVIEW

Security in the Taiwan Strait is largely a function of dynamic interactions between and among mainland China, Taiwan, and the United States. China's strategy toward Taiwan has been influenced by what it sees as positive developments in Taiwan's political situation and approach to engagement with China. The two sides have made progress in expanding cross-Strait trade and economic links and people-to-people contacts. However, China's overall strategy continues to incorporate elements of persuasion and coercion to deter or repress the development of political attitudes in Taiwan favoring independence.

Despite positive public statements about cross-Strait dynamics from top leaders in China following the re-election of Taiwan President Ma Ying-jeou in 2012, there have been no signs that China's military disposition opposite Taiwan has changed significantly. The PLA has continued to develop and deploy military capabilities to coerce Taiwan or to attempt an invasion, if necessary. In particular, the MISSION ACTION 2013 large-scale joint exercises seen may have been designed to develop the integrated operational capabilities necessary for a cross-Strait invasion of Taiwan. These improvements pose major challenges to Taiwan's security, which has historically been based upon the PLA's inability to project power across the 100-nm-wide Taiwan Strait due to natural geographic advantages of island defense, Taiwan's armed forces' technological superiority, and the possibility of U.S. intervention.

CHINA'S STRATEGY IN THE TAIWAN STRAIT

China appears prepared to defer the use of force as long as it believes that unification over the long term remains possible and the costs of conflict outweigh the benefits. China argues that the credible threat of use of force is essential to maintain the conditions for political progress and to prevent Taiwan from making moves toward *de jure* independence. China has refused for decades to renounce the use of force to resolve the Taiwan issue, despite simultaneously professing its desire for peaceful unification under the principle of "one country, two systems."

The circumstances under which the mainland has historically warned it would use force have evolved over time in response to the island's declarations of its political status, changes in PLA capabilities, and China's view of Taiwan's relations with other countries. These circumstances, or "red lines," have included:

> Formal declaration of Taiwan independence;

> Undefined moves toward Taiwan independence;

> Internal unrest on Taiwan;

> Taiwan's acquisition of nuclear weapons;

> Indefinite delays in the resumption of cross-Strait dialogue on unification;

> Foreign intervention in Taiwan's internal affairs; and,

> Foreign forces stationed on Taiwan.

Article 8 of the March 2005 "Anti-Secession Law" states that China may use "non-peaceful means" if "secessionist forces … cause the fact of Taiwan's secession from China"; if "major incidents entailing Taiwan's secession" occur; or, if "possibilities for peaceful reunification" are exhausted. The ambiguity of these "red lines" preserves China's flexibility.

CHINA'S COURSES OF ACTION AGAINST TAIWAN

The PLA is capable of increasingly sophisticated military action against Taiwan. It is possible China would first pursue a measured approach characterized by signaling its readiness to use force, followed by a deliberate buildup of force to optimize the speed of engagement over strategic deception. Another option is that China would sacrifice overt, large-scale preparations in favor of surprise to force rapid military or political resolution before other countries could respond. If a quick resolution is not possible, China would seek to:

> Deter potential U.S. intervention;

> Failing that, delay intervention and seek victory in an asymmetric, limited, quick war; and,

> Fight to a standstill and pursue a political settlement after a protracted conflict.

Maritime Quarantine or Blockade. In addition to direct military engagement, PLA writings describe potential alternative solutions—air blockades, missile attacks, and mining to force capitulation. China could declare that ships en route to Taiwan must stop in mainland ports for inspection or transshipment prior to transiting to Taiwan ports. China could also attempt the equivalent of a blockade by declaring exercise or missile closure areas in approaches to ports, in effect closing port access and diverting merchant traffic. The PLA employed this method during the 1995 to 1996 missile firings and live-fire exercises. There is a risk, however, that China would underestimate the degree to which any attempt to limit maritime traffic to and from Taiwan would trigger countervailing international pressure and military escalation. China today probably could not enforce a full military blockade. However, its ability to do so will improve significantly over the next five to ten years.

Limited Force or Coercive Options. China might use a variety of disruptive, punitive, or lethal military actions in a limited campaign against Taiwan, likely in conjunction with overt and clandestine economic and political activities. Such a campaign could include computer network or limited kinetic attacks against Taiwan's political, military, and economic infrastructure to induce fear in Taiwan and degrade the populace's confidence in the Taiwan leadership. Similarly,

PLA special operations forces could infiltrate Taiwan and conduct attacks against infrastructure or leadership targets.

Air and Missile Campaign. China could use missile attacks and precision strikes against air defense systems, including air bases, radar sites, missiles, space assets, and communications facilities to degrade Taiwan's defenses, neutralize Taiwan's leadership, or break the Taiwan people's will to fight.

Amphibious Invasion. Publicly available Chinese writings describe different operational concepts for amphibious invasion. The most prominent of these, the Joint Island Landing Campaign, envisions a complex operation relying on coordinated, interlocking campaigns for logistics, air, and naval support, and electronic warfare. The objective would be to break through or circumvent shore defenses, establish and build a beachhead, transport personnel and materiel to designated landing sites in the north or south of Taiwan's western coastline, and launch attacks to seize and occupy key targets or the entire island.

The PLA is capable of accomplishing various amphibious operations short of a full-scale invasion of Taiwan. With few overt military preparations beyond routine training, China could launch an invasion of small Taiwan-held islands in the South China Sea such as Pratas or Itu Aba. A PLA invasion of a medium-sized, better defended offshore island such as Matsu or Jinmen is within China's capabilities. Such an invasion would demonstrate military capability and political resolve while achieving tangible territorial gain and simultaneously showing some measure of restraint. However, this kind of operation includes significant, if not prohibitive, political risk because it could galvanize pro-independence sentiment on Taiwan and generate international opposition.

Large-scale amphibious invasion is one of the most complicated and difficult military operations the PLA might pursue in a cross-Strait contingency. Success would depend upon air and sea superiority, rapid buildup and sustainment of supplies on shore, and uninterrupted support. An attempt to invade Taiwan would strain China's armed forces and invite international intervention. These stresses, combined with China's combat force attrition and the complexity of urban warfare and counterinsurgency, assuming a successful landing and breakout, make amphibious invasion of Taiwan a significant political and military risk. Taiwan's investments to harden infrastructure and strengthen defensive capabilities could also decrease China's ability to achieve its objectives. Moreover, China does not appear to be building the conventional amphibious lift required to support such a campaign.

THE PLA'S CURRENT POSTURE FOR A TAIWAN CONFLICT

Preparation for a Taiwan conflict with the possibility of U.S. involvement continues to dominate China's military modernization program.

Missile Forces. The Second Artillery is prepared to conduct missile attacks and precision strikes against Taiwan's air defense systems, air bases, radar sites, missiles, space assets, and C2 and communications facilities, in an attempt to degrade Taiwan's defenses, neutralize Taiwan's leadership, or break the public's will to fight.

Air Forces. The PLA Air Force has maintained a force posture that provides it with a variety of capabilities to leverage against Taiwan in a contingency. First, it has stationed a large number of advanced aircraft within an unrefueled range of Taiwan, providing a significant capability to conduct air superiority and ground attack operations against Taiwan. Second, a number of long-range air defense systems provide a strong layer of defense of China's mainland against a counterattack. Third, China's development of support aircraft provide it improved ISR to enable PLAAF operations in a contingency.

Navy Forces. The PLA Navy is improving anti-air and anti-surface warfare capabilities, developing a credible at-sea nuclear deterrent, and introducing new platforms that are positioned to strike Taiwan in a cross-Strait conflict. The additional attack submarines, multi-mission surface combatants, and fourth-generation naval aircraft entering the force are designed to achieve sea superiority within the first island chain as well as deter and counter any potential third-party intervention in a Taiwan conflict. The PLA Navy currently

lacks the amphibious lift capacity that a large-scale invasion of Taiwan would require.

Ground Forces. Increasingly armed with more modern systems such as armed attack helicopters, the PLA ground forces are conducting joint training exercises that will prepare them for a Taiwan invasion scenario. Training, including amphibious landing training, is often conducted under realistic conditions, including all-weather and at night. Improved networks provide real-time data transmissions within and between units, enabling better C2 during operations. Additionally, the PLA Army's ongoing fielding of advanced air defense equipment is significantly enhancing the self-defense of key C2 elements and other critical assets assessed as likely tasked for potential use against Taiwan. As the number of these new systems grows in the PLA ground forces, the ability of an amphibious invasion force to successfully defend cross-Strait amphibious lodgments against counterattacks by both legacy and advanced weaponry will inevitably increase.

TAIWAN'S DEFENSIVE CAPABILITIES

Taiwan has historically relied upon multiple military variables to deter PLA aggression: the PLA's inability to project sufficient power across the 100-mile-wide Taiwan Strait, the Taiwan military's technological superiority, and the inherent geographic advantages of island defense. China's increasingly modern weapons and platforms (more than 1,200 ballistic missiles, an anti-ship ballistic missile program, ships and submarines, combat aircraft, and improved C4ISR capabilities) have eroded or negated many of these factors.

Taiwan has taken important steps to build its war reserve stocks, grown its defense industrial base, improved joint operations and crisis response capabilities, and increased its officer and non-commissioned officer (NCO) corps. These improvements partially address Taiwan's declining defensive advantages. Taiwan is following through with its transition to an all-volunteer military and reducing its active military end-strength from 275,000 to approximately 175,000 personnel to create a "small but smart and strong force." Recognizing the continued growth in China's military spending, Taiwan is working to integrate innovative and asymmetric measures into its defense planning in order to counterbalance China's growing capabilities.

U.S. policy toward Taiwan derives from its one-China policy, based on the three U.S.-China Joint Communiqués and the Taiwan Relations Act (TRA). U.S. policy opposes any destabilizing unilateral changes to the status quo in the Taiwan Strait by either side. The United States continues to support peaceful resolution of cross-Strait differences in a manner acceptable to the people on both sides.

Consistent with the TRA, the United States has helped to maintain peace, security, and stability in the Taiwan Strait by providing defense articles and services to enable Taiwan to maintain a sufficient self-defense capability. To this end, the United States has announced more than $12 billion in arms sales to Taiwan since 2010. This includes, most recently, in September 2011, an advanced retrofit program for Taiwan's F-16 A/B fighter jets, training, and spare parts for Taiwan's air force.

6

U.S.-CHINA
MILITARY-TO-MILITARY CONTACTS

STRATEGY FOR ENGAGEMENT

During their June 2013 Sunnylands summit, U.S. President Barack Obama and PRC President Xi Jinping emphasized the importance of developing a new model of bilateral relations that avoids the historical trap of conflict between a rising power and an established one, preventing the relationship from unnecessarily deteriorating into strategic rivalry. Both sides have articulated the desire for a new model of military-to-military relations that is an integral part of a broader shared vision for a positive, cooperative, and comprehensive U.S.-China relationship.

The U.S. DoD's approach to military engagement with the PRC's Ministry of National Defense focuses on three lines of effort: building cooperative capacity in areas of mutual interest; fostering greater institutional understanding; and promoting common views of the regional security environment and related security challenges. In 2014, the DoD will pursue these lines of effort to develop a "new model of military-to-military relations" focused on: sustained, substantive dialogue; concrete, practical cooperation; and enhanced risk reduction.

The U.S.-China relationship has elements of both cooperation and competition. A new model of military-to-military relations seeks to manage competition through sustained and substantive dialogue and a commitment to risk reduction, and at the same time deepen practical, concrete cooperation in areas of mutual interest. The relationships and channels of communication developed through military-to-military engagements are particularly important during periods of tension, and contacts at all levels can help reduce miscommunication, misunderstanding, and the risks of miscalculation.

The pace and scope of China's military modernization over the past two decades provide opportunities for cooperation. At the same time, as China's military modernizes its capabilities and expands its presence in Asia, the risk of an accident or miscalculation also increases, which places a premium on risk reduction efforts.

President Obama stressed that the United States' future depends on a peaceful and prosperous Asia. Pursuit of a positive and constructive relationship with China is an important part of the U.S. rebalance, which is designed to preserve and enhance stability in the international system and the Asia-Pacific region. Sustaining the positive momentum in the military-to-military relationship supports U.S. policy objectives of promoting China's development in a manner consistent with international rules and norms and that serves as a source of security and shared prosperity in Asia.

MILITARY-TO-MILITARY ENGAGEMENT IN 2013 – HIGHLIGHTS

Throughout the course of the past year, the DoD has made progress with the PLA in developing cooperative capacity in areas of mutual interest, including HA/DR, counterpiracy, search and rescue, and military medicine. The Department of Defense conducts all contacts with China in a manner consistent with the provisions of the National Defense Authorization Act (NDAA) for FY 2000.

Selected visits, exchanges, and exercises in 2013 are highlighted below, and a complete list of 2013 engagements is provided at Appendix I.

High-Level Visits. High-level contacts are an important means to exchange views on the international security environment, to identify areas of common perspective, and to facilitate common approaches to shared challenges.

In April, U.S. Chairman of the Joint Chiefs of Staff General Martin Dempsey traveled to China, where he met with senior military leaders in Beijing and observed a Z-10 attack helicopter flight demonstration at the 4th Aviation Regiment, visited the PLA Aviation Academy, and spoke with command and senior staff officers at the PRC National Defense University (NDU).

In August, PRC Minister of National Defense General Chang Wanquan visited the United States, making stops at U.S. Pacific Command Headquarters in Honolulu, Hawaii, and U.S. Northern Command Headquarters in Colorado Springs, Colorado, and meeting with Secretary of Defense Chuck Hagel in Washington, D.C.

In September, PLA Navy Commander Admiral Wu Shengli traveled to the United States, visiting U.S. Naval Base San Diego where he toured the USS CARL VINSON (CVN-70), the USS FORT WORTH (LCS-3), and the USS JEFFERSON CITY (SSN-759), and visited Washington, D.C., where he had meetings at the Pentagon with Chief of Naval Operations Admiral Jonathan Greenert and other senior officials and toured Walter Reed National Medical Center.

Later in September, Chief of Staff of the Air Force General Mark Welsh visited China, where had meetings in Beijing, visited the Jianqiao Air Base in Hangzhou, and toured the Civil Aviation Department Headquarters and Shek Kong Air Base in Hong Kong.

In November, PRC Beijing Military Region Commander Lieutenant General Zhang Shibo visited the United States, making stops in New York, Washington, D.C., and U.S. Northern Command Headquarters in Colorado Springs, Colorado.

Recurrent Exchanges. Recurring, institutionalized events form the backbone of U.S.-China defense policy discussions each year. They serve as a regularized, routine mechanism for dialogue.

In July, on the margins of the Strategic and Economic Dialogue (S&ED) in Washington, D.C., then-Under Secretary of Defense for Policy Dr. James Miller participated in the Department of State-led third annual Strategic Security Dialogue (SSD). Under Secretary Miller also led the DoD delegation to the S&ED, where he spoke at the final Strategic Track plenary session on the state of U.S.-China military-to-military relations. Under Secretary Miller's PRC counterpart, Deputy Chief of the General Staff Lieutenant General Wang Guanzhong, also participated in both the SSD and the S&ED.

In August, the USPACOM-led Military Maritime Consultative Agreement (MMCA) working group and plenary session took place in Honolulu, Hawaii, with a preparatory working group meeting in China in May. The meetings focused on humanitarian assistance, disaster relief, and maritime safety.

In September, Under Secretary Miller led the annual Defense Consultative Talks (DCTs) in Beijing. The DCTs are the highest-level annual defense dialogue between the United States and China. The 2013 talks focused on specific ways to maintain momentum in advancing a new model of U.S.-China military-to-military relations, particularly through sustained, substantive dialogue; concrete and practical cooperation; and, expanding opportunities to reduce the risk of misperception, misunderstanding or miscalculation in key strategic areas.

In December, the two sides conducted the annual Defense Policy Coordination Talks (DPCTs) in Beijing. The Deputy Assistant Secretary-led DPCTs focused on maritime safety and security, as well as regional and global security issues, and also served as the key forum for beginning negotiations on the 2014 military-to-military engagement plan.

Academic and Functional Exchanges. Reciprocal exchanges between mid-grade and junior officers and institutions of professional military education cultivate a generation of rising leaders on both sides who are adept at handling this increasingly complex and vital relationship.

In April 2013, Secretary of State John Kerry announced that the United States and China had agreed to establish an interagency cyber working group under the auspices of the ongoing bilateral Strategic Security Dialogue. During the Sunnylands summit in June 2013, Presidents Obama and Xi agreed on the need for rules and common approaches to cybersecurity in order to build trust and reduce the risk of miscalculation, misinterpretation, and escalation. Two meetings of the cyber working group took place in 2013. Through this mechanism, the United States seeks substantive dialogue with counterparts across China's government on cyber issues.

In May, USS SHILOH (CG 65) conducted the first port visit to China since April 2009. Events during the port call included reciprocal receptions, tours, a community relations visit to a school, and sporting events. Additionally, in conjunction with the ship visit, ADM Haney, then Commander, U.S. Pacific Fleet (PACFLT), conducted the first visit by a PACFLT Commander to China since November 2006. ADM Haney met with LTG Qi Jianguo, Deputy Chief of the General Staff, in Beijing;ADM Wu Shengli, Commander, PLA Navy, in Beijing; and VADM Jiang Weilie, South Sea Fleet Commander, in Zhanjiang.

In June, the inaugural U.S.-China Maritime Legal Issues Working Group was held in the United States. The goal of the working group was to clarify both sides' positions on a range of maritime legal issues in an effort to improve mutual understanding. A central discussion topic was the conduct of military activities in an Exclusive Economic Zone (EEZ).

In June, U.S. Navy and PLA Navy forces participated in the ADMM-Plus Humanitarian Assistance/Disaster Relief and Military Medicine Exercises hosted in Brunei. The PLA Navy forces included its hospital ship, the ANWEI-class PEACE ARK.

In July 2013, four Chinese midshipmen from Dalian Naval Academy participated in the U.S. Naval Academy's Yard Patrol (YP) Craft orientation and familiarization program.

In August, the United States and China conducted their second bilateral counterpiracy exercise in the Gulf of Aden.

In September, a PLA Navy Task Force led by RADM Wei Gang, Chief of Staff, North Sea Fleet, and consisting of three ships (QINGDAO (DD113), LINYI (FFG 547), and HONGZEHU (AOR 881)) conducted a port visit to Pearl Harbor, Hawaii. China's Ambassador to the United States., Cui Tiankai, also attended. Events during the port call were hosted by USS LAKE ERIE (CG 70) and included reciprocal receptions, tours, sporting events, damage control equipment demonstration, a search and rescue table-top exercise, a communications exercise, and a search and rescue exercise.

In November, Vice Chief of Naval Operations Admiral Mark Ferguson led a Senior Leader Familiarization Visit to China. The delegation members participated in meetings in Beijing and visited Zhoushan Naval Base, where they toured a JIANGKAI II-class guided missile frigate and a YUAN-class attack submarine.

In December, the United States and China conducted a Disaster Management Exchange (DME) in Hawaii to build capacity for U.S.-

China cooperation in HA/DR through defense support to civil authorities in the event of a disaster. The event marked the first time PLA troops exercised on U.S. soil.

PLANNING FOR MILITARY-TO-MILITARY ENGAGEMENTS IN 2014

Planning for 2014 military-to-military engagements began during the DPCTs in December 2013. As this report went to print, the 2014 plan had been agreed to in principle. A list of planned engagements for 2014 is provided in Appendix I.

SPECIAL TOPIC: RECONNAISSANCE SATELLITES

China has developed a large constellation of imaging and remote sensing satellites. These satellites can support military objectives by providing situational awareness of foreign military force deployments, critical infrastructure, and targets of political significance.

> Since 2006, China has conducted 18 Yaogan remote sensing satellite launches. The Yaogan satellites conduct scientific experiments, carry out surveys on land resources, estimate crop yield, and support natural disaster reduction and prevention.

> China launched the Gaofen-1 satellite in April 2013. The Gaofen program is one of 16 programs announced by the State Council for its national scientific and technology programs. Gaofen will become the main civilian Earth observation project, combining the use of satellites, aircraft, and even stratosphere balloons, with at least 14 satellites set to launch by 2020. Gaofen-2 is expected to launch this year.

> The Kuaizhou ("quick vessel") imagery satellite was launched on September 25, 2013. Kuaizhou-1 was built by the Harbin Institute of Technology and is projected to be used for emergency data monitoring and imaging under the control of the Chinese Academy of Sciences' National Remote Sensing Center.

> Additionally, China has launched two Tianhui satellites designed to conduct scientific experiments and support land resource surveys and territory mapping with a stereoscopic imaging payload.

> China has three Huanjing disaster monitoring satellites currently on orbit (the third of which was launched in November 2012).

> The Ziyuan series of satellites are used for earth resources, cartography, surveying, and monitoring.

> China also operates the Haiyang ocean monitoring constellation and Fengyun weather satellites in low Earth and geosynchronous orbits.

China plans to continue to increase its on-orbit constellation with the launch of 100 satellites through 2015. The future launches will include imaging, remote sensing, navigation, communication, and scientific satellites, as well as manned spacecraft.

SPECIAL TOPIC: CHINA'S USE OF LOW-OBSERVABLE TECHNOLOGY

For decades, the PLA has been incorporating low-observable technology into each of its services to suppress signals from its weapons and equipment that can be exploited by high-technology militaries to locate and target Chinese forces. PLA doctrinal publications, such as the 2009 *Science of Army Operations,* suggest that the PLA considers low-observable technologies as part of a broader suite of information countermeasures, specifically referring to it as a type of radar jamming:

> "There are two major forms of information countermeasures as far as effects are relevant .... Radar jamming is meant to mainly weaken or destroy the normal operating capability of the enemy's radar system by irradiating or transmitting jamming electromagnetic waves through radar jamming equipment; or **use equipment that does not produce electromagnetic radiation by itself to reflect, scatter, or absorb electromagnetic waves transmitted from enemy radar so as to prevent the enemy radar from detecting and tracking real targets** or causing mistakes in the enemy radar." [Emphasis added.]

New weapons and equipment that use low-observable technology that were demonstrated in 2013 include:

> In February 2013, the PLA Navy launched the first ship in the new Type 056 class of corvettes, which incorporates stealth features making it more difficult to detect using radar. Although these ships can fulfill a variety of missions, they increase the PLA Navy's ability to impose a naval blockade on Taiwan.

> After four years in development, in November 2013, the PLA flight tested its new stealth drone, the Lijian, which a Chinese news source described as "highly maneuverable and capable in air-to-air combat."

> In July the PLA, which has long used camouflage, introduced a new type of camouflage netting that has multiple layers of special paints, digital camouflage, and the ability to counter detection from infrared, thermal imaging and radar reconnaissance sensors.

> Throughout 2013, the PLA Air Force continued testing its two fifth-generation stealth fighters—the J-20 and the J-31.

PLA Stealth Aircraft. The PLA seeks to develop aircraft with low observable features, advanced avionics, super-cruise engines, and stealth applications as demonstrated by the January 2011 flight test of the J-20 prototype and recent observations of a second indigenously produced aircraft with stealth features, referred to as the J-31. China seeks to develop these advanced aircraft to improve its regional power projection capabilities and strengthen its ability to strike regional airbases and facilities. China's first fifth-generation fighter, the multi-role J-20, is not expected to enter service prior to 2018, and China faces numerous challenges to achieving full operational capability, including developing high-performance jet engines. China's second fifth-generation fighter, the smaller but likely also multi-role, J-31, conducted its first flight in October 2012. The PLA Air Force has observed how foreign militaries employ stealth aircraft and views this technology as critical to its transformation from a predominantly territorial air force to one capable of conducting both offensive and defensive operations. The PLA Air Force believes that stealth provides an offensive operational advantage that denies an adversary the time to mobilize and conduct defensive operations.

SPECIAL TOPIC: CHINA'S FIRST AIRCRAFT CARRIER

The most significant development in the PLA Navy over the past year has been the first long-range deployment and continued flight operations of China's first aircraft carrier, CV-16, the LIAONING. The LIAONING was commissioned and entered service with the PLA Navy on September 25, 2012. The carrier most likely will conduct extensive local operations focusing on shipboard training, carrier aircraft integration, and carrier formation training for the next three to four years. The carrier conducted operations in the East China Sea and South China Sea in November may be used for other missions as needed.

The carrier will be based at Yuchi in the Qingdao area at least for the near term, although Sanya Naval Base on Hainan Island is a future possibility, particularly after an operational air wing is formed. The base at Yuchi features a deep draft harbor with replenishment, repair, and maintenance facilities. The Qingdao area also supports nearby airfields for aircraft maintenance and repair.

The J-15, a carrier-based fighter modeled after the Russian Su-33, conducted its first takeoffs and landings from the LIAONING on November 26, 2012. By September 2013, J-15s were conducting full-stops and takeoffs with weapon loads at full maximum gross weights. Additional full-stop landings, ramp takeoffs, and storage of aircraft in the hangar bay below the flight deck continued in October. Although the J-15 has a land-based combat radius of 1,200 km, the aircraft will be limited in range and armament when operating from the carrier, because the ski-jump design does not provide as much airspeed and, therefore, lift at takeoff as a catapult design.

China acknowledged publicly for the first time in 2013 its desire to build indigenous aircraft carriers. The first Chinese-built carrier will likely be operational sometime at the beginning of the next decade. The formation of carrier battle groups will enable the PLA Navy to conduct comprehensive sea control and power projection operations and enhance its long-range operational capabilities.

SPECIAL TOPIC: INTEGRATED AIR DEFENSES

China has developed a national integrated air defense system (IADS) to defend key strategic cities and borders, territorial claims. Overall, China's IADS represents a multilayered defense consisting of weapon systems, radars, and C4ISR platforms working together to counter air threats at various ranges and altitudes. One of China's primary goals is to defend against precision strike munitions such as cruise and ballistic missiles, especially those launched from long distances. Defense against stealth aircraft and unmanned aerial vehicles is also a growing priority.

Air Defense Weapons. China's air force and navy employ land- and sea-based SAMs and air defense artillery (ADA), and its ground forces employ short- and medium-range SAMs and ADA in extensive numbers. The PLA Air Force employs one of the largest forces of advanced SAMs, including Russian-built SA-20 (S-300 PMU1/PMU2) and domestically produced CSA-9 (HQ-9) battalions. China has shown interest in Russia's newest long-range SAM, the SA-X-21b (S-400) TRIUMF, but a contract has not been signed. Russian officials have stated China would not receive the S-400 until at least 2017. This SAM can target aircraft, cruise missiles, and tactical and medium-range ballistic missiles.

Early Warning Network. Another element of China's multilayered IADS is its extensive ground-based radar network. In the past, this ground-based early warning network and China's Russian-acquired SAMs primarily protected Beijing and other key strategic locations in the eastern part of the country. China has since developed the KONGJING-2000 (KJ-2000) airborne early warning aircraft to provide coverage at long ranges and low altitudes for faster response and command targeting to weapon systems. In the future, China may expand its national early warning network to protect China's territorial air space and waters farther from the mainland, as well as to provide space defense. This effort would include China's growing constellation of reconnaissance, data relay, navigation, and communications satellites. China is also improving reconnaissance technologies to include infrared, multiple-spectrum, pulsed Doppler, phased array, and passive detection. Over-the-horizon skywave radar is also an important component of China's improvement in its strategic early warning capabilities.

C4ISR Network. China's IADS also includes a C4ISR network to connect early warning platforms, SAM and ADA, and command posts to improve communication and response time during operations. The network is intended to include battle damage assessment capability. China continues to make progress on command, communication, and control systems. China's air defense brigades are training to use this information network and mobile command and control platforms to connect the operations of different types of weapon systems by sending automated targeting information to them simultaneously. China is also using simulation systems to attempt to train for command of air defense operations in realistic operational conditions, including network warfare. China has deployed air defense brigades employing its newest SAM system to the western part of China to train for long-distance mobility and operations in high-altitude conditions, including operations under the conditions of network warfare.

APPENDIX I: MILITARY-TO-MILITARY EXCHANGES

U.S.-CHINA MILITARY-TO-MILITARY CONTACTS FOR 2013	
HIGH-LEVEL VISITS TO CHINA	*Month (2013)*
Chairman of the Joint Chiefs of Staff to China	April
Chief of Staff of the Air Force to China	September
HIGH-LEVEL VISITS TO UNITED STATES	
PRC Minister of National Defense to United States	August
PRC PLA Navy Commander to United States	September
PRC Beijing Military Region Commander to United States	November
RECURRENT EXCHANGES	
Military Maritime Consultative Agreement (MMCA) Working Group #1 in China	May
USN Ship and PACFLT Commander Visit to China	May
Maritime Legal Issues Working Group in the United States	June
Defense Consultative Talks in China	September
MMCA Working Group #2 and Plenary Session in the United States	September
Defense Policy Coordination Talks in China	December
ACADEMIC EXCHANGES	
PLA Cadets Participate in USMA Sandhurst Competition in United States	April
PRC National Defense University "Dragons" delegation to United States	May
PLAN Midshipmen Participate in USNA Yard Patrol Craft Program in United States	July
PRC National Defense University "Tigers" delegation to United States	October
FUNCTIONAL EXCHANGES	
PLA Daily Media Outreach delegation to the United States	January
PLA Senior Leader Familiarization Visit to the United States	March
PLA Doctrine Delegation to the U.S. Command and General Staff College	September
Defense POW/Missing Personnel Office meeting with PLA Archivists in China	October
Vice Chief of Naval Operations-led Senior Leader Familiarization Visit to China	November
JOINT EXERCISES	
Gulf of Aden (GOA) Counter-piracy Exercise	August
Search and Rescue Exercise during PLA Navy ship visit in United States	September

U.S.-CHINA MILITARY-TO-MILITARY EXCHANGES PLANNED FOR 2014

HIGH-LEVEL VISITS TO CHINA

Secretary of Defense to China

Chief of Staff of the Army to China

Chief of Naval Operations to China

Commandant of the Marine Corps to China

Commander, U.S. Pacific Command, to China

Commander, U.S. Northern Command, to China

HIGH-LEVEL VISITS TO UNITED STATES

PLA Chief of the General Staff to United States

Nanjing Military Region Air Force Commander to United States

PRC Senior Military Delegation to United States (TBD)

RECURRENT EXCHANGES

Defense Consultative Talks

Defense Policy Coordination Talks

MMCA Plenary and Working Groups

Maritime Legal Issues Working Group

PLA Navy Ship Visit to United States

USN Ship Visit to China

Defense POW/MIA Office – PLA Archivists Meeting

ACADEMIC EXCHANGES

U.S. National Defense University- PRC National Defense University Strategic Dialogue

PRC National Defense University "Dragons" delegation to United States

Academy of Military Science / Army War College Exchange to United States

U.S. National Defense University "Capstone" delegation to China

National War College student delegation to China

PLA Navy War College visit to United States

U.S. Naval War College visit to China

PLA Air Force Command College visit to United States

U.S. Air War College visit to China

West Point Superintendent visit to PLA University of Science and Technology

U.S. Naval Academy Superintendent visit to Dalian Naval Academy

PRC Army cadet participation in West Point's International Week/Sandhurst competition*

PLA Navy midshipmen participation in USNA Yard Patrol Craft program*

PLA Air Force cadets to Air Force Academy Fall International Week*

FUNCTIONAL EXCHANGES

PLA Senior Leader Familiarization Course

U.S. Senior Leader Familiarization Course

PLA Navy Senior Officer Familiarization visit to Untied States

PLA Mid and Junior Officer Familiarization Delegation to United States

PACOM Mid-Level Officer Familiarization Delegation to China

Human Resources Management Study Group

PRC Peacekeeping Delegation to Carlisle Barracks, PA

Military Environmental Protection Delegation

PLA Military Medical Delegation

Military Legal Issues Study Group

OSD Public Affairs Delegation to China

JOINT EXERCISES

Gulf of Aden Counter-piracy Exercise

Disaster Management Exchange and Humanitarian Assistance/Disaster Relief Field Exchange in China

Rim of the Pacific (RIMPAC) Exercise 2014*

Search and Rescue Exercise(s) in conjunction with ship visit(s)

*Denotes multilateral event

BILATERAL OR MULTILATERAL MILITARY EXERCISES INVOLVING THE PLA 2008-2013

Bilateral and Multilateral Exercises Since 2008			
Year	**Exercise Name**	**Type of Exercise**	**Participants**
2008	Hand-in-Hand 2008	Counterterrorism	India
	Strike 2008	Counterterrorism	Thailand
2009	Aman (Peace) 2009	Maritime	Hosted by Pakistan (38 countries participated)
	Cooperation 2009	Counterterrorism	Singapore
	Country-Gate Sharp Sword 2009	Counterterrorism	Russia
	Peace Angel 2009	Medical	Gabon
	Peace Keeping Mission 2009	Peacekeeping Operations	Mongolia
	Peace Mission 2009	Counterterrorism	Russia
	Peace Shield 2009	Counter-Piracy	Russia
	Unnamed	Maritime	Singapore
2010	Blue Strike/Blue Assault 2010	Counterterrorism	Thailand
	Cooperation 2010	Counterterrorism	Singapore
	Friendship 2010	Counterterrorism	Pakistan
	Friendship Action 2010	Ground (Mountain Warfare)	Romania
	Peace Angel 2010	Medical	Peru
	Peace Mission 2010	Counterterrorism	Russia, Kazakhstan, Kyrgyzstan, Tajikistan
	Strike 2010	Counterterrorism	Thailand
	Unnamed	Search and Rescue	Australia
	Unnamed	Maritime	New Zealand
	Unnamed	Counter-Piracy	South Korea
	Unnamed	Search and Rescue	Taiwan
	Unnamed	Air	Turkey
	Unnamed	Ground	Turkey
	Unnamed	Search and Rescue	Vietnam
	Unnamed	Joint Border Patrol	Kazakhstan
	Shaheen 1	Air Exercise	Pakistan
2011	Tian Shan-2 2011	Counterterrorism	Kazakhstan, Kyrgyzstan, Russia, Tajikistan, Uzbekistan
	Aman (Peace) 2011	Maritime	Hosted by Pakistan (39 countries participated)
	Unnamed	Maritime (Counterpiracy)	Tanzania
	Unnamed	Maritime (Counterpiracy)	Pakistan
	Sharp Blade-2011	Special Operations/Counterterrorism	Indonesia
	Unnamed	Maritime	Vietnam
	Unnamed	Airborne	Belarus
	Khan Quest-11	Peacekeeping Operations (observer status)	Mongolia

Year	Exercise	Type	Countries
	Cooperation-2011	Special Operations (Urban Warfare)	Venezuela
	Friendship-IV	Ground (Low Intensity Conflict)	Pakistan
	Cooperation Spirit 2011	Humanitarian Aid/Disaster Relief	Australia
2012	Naval Cooperation 2012	Maritime	Russia
	Unnamed	Counter-Piracy	France
	Blue Assault 2012	Maritime (Amphibious Assault)	Thailand
	Peace Mission 2012	Counterterrorism	Kazakhstan, Kyrgyzstan, Russia, Tajikistan, Uzbekistan
	Sharp Knife 2012	Counterterrorism	Indonesia
	Unnamed	Maritime (Search and Rescue)	Vietnam
	Unnamed	Counterpiracy	United States
	Cooperation Spirit 2012	HA/DR	Australia, New Zealand
	Khan Quest-12	Peacekeeping Operations (observer status)	Mongolia
2013	-*Unnamed* 2013	Counterterrorism	Pakistan
	-ADMM+ Exercise in Brunei 2013	Maritime (Search and Rescue), HA/DR	ASEAN
	-Peace Mission 2013	Counterterrorism	Russia
	-Frontier Defense Joint Determination 2013	Counterterrorism	Kyrgyzstan
	-Sharp Knife 2013	Counterterrorism	Indonesia
	-Hand in Hand 2013	Counterterrorism	India
	Khan Quest-13	Peacekeeping Operations (observer status)	Mongolia
	-Strike 2013	Counterterrorism	Thailand

APPENDIX II: CHINA AND TAIWAN FORCES DATA

Taiwan Strait Military Balance, Ground Forces			
	China		**Taiwan**
	Total	*Taiwan Strait Area*	*Total*
Personnel (Active)	1.25 million	400,000	130,000
Group Armies	18	8	3
Infantry Divisions	15	5	0
Infantry Brigades	16	6	8
Mechanized Infantry Divisions	6	2	0
Mechanized Infantry Brigades	17	7	3
Armor Divisions	1	0	0
Armor Brigades	16	7	4
Artillery Divisions	2	2	0
Artillery Brigades	17	6	5
Airborne Divisions	3	3	0
Amphibious Divisions	2	2	0
Amphibious Brigades	3	3	3
Tanks	7,000	3,000	1,100
Artillery Pieces	8,000	3,000	1,600

Note: PLA active ground forces are organized into Group Armies. Infantry, armor, and artillery units are organized into a combination of divisions and brigades deployed throughout the PLA's seven MRs. A significant portion of these assets are deployed in the Taiwan Strait area, specifically the Nanjing, Guangzhou, and Jinan MRs. Taiwan has seven Defense Commands, three of which have Field Armies. Each Army contains an Artillery Command roughly equivalent to a brigade plus.

Taiwan Strait Military Balance, Naval Forces			
	China		Taiwan
	Total	East and South Sea Fleets	Total
Aircraft Carriers	1	0	0
Destroyers	24	14	4
Frigates	49	40	22
Corvettes	8	6	0
Tank Landing Ships/ Amphibious Transport Dock	29	26	12
Medium Landing Ships	28	21	4
Diesel Attack Submarines	51	32	4
Nuclear Attack Submarines	5	2	0
Coastal Patrol (Missile)	85	67	45

Note: The PLA Navy has the largest force of principal combatants, submarines, and amphibious warfare ships in Asia. In the event of a major Taiwan conflict, the East and South Sea Fleets would be expected to participate in direct action against the Taiwan Navy. The North Sea Fleet would be responsible primarily for protecting Beijing and the northern coast, but could provide mission-critical assets to support other fleets.

Taiwan Strait Military Balance, Air Forces			
	China		Taiwan
Aircraft	Total	Within range of Taiwan	Total
Fighters	1,700	130	388
Bombers/Attack	400	200	22
Transport	475	150*	21

Note: The PLAAF and the PLA Navy have approximately 2,100 operational combat aircraft. These consist of air defense and multi-role fighters, ground attack aircraft, fighter-bombers, and bombers. An additional 1,450 older fighters, bombers, and trainers are employed for training and research and development. The two air arms also possess approximately 475 transports and more than 100 surveillance and reconnaissance aircraft with intelligence, surface search, and airborne early warning capabilities. The PLAAF would likely supplement its military transports with civilian aircraft in a combat scenario. The majority of PLAAF and PLA Navy aircraft are based in the eastern half of the country. Currently, 330 aircraft could conduct combat operations against Taiwan without refueling. However, this number could be significantly increased through any combination of aircraft forward deployment, decreased ordnance loads, or altered mission profiles.

* This number is 250 aircraft fewer than last year's transport total, but reflects a change in methodology versus aircraft acquisition.

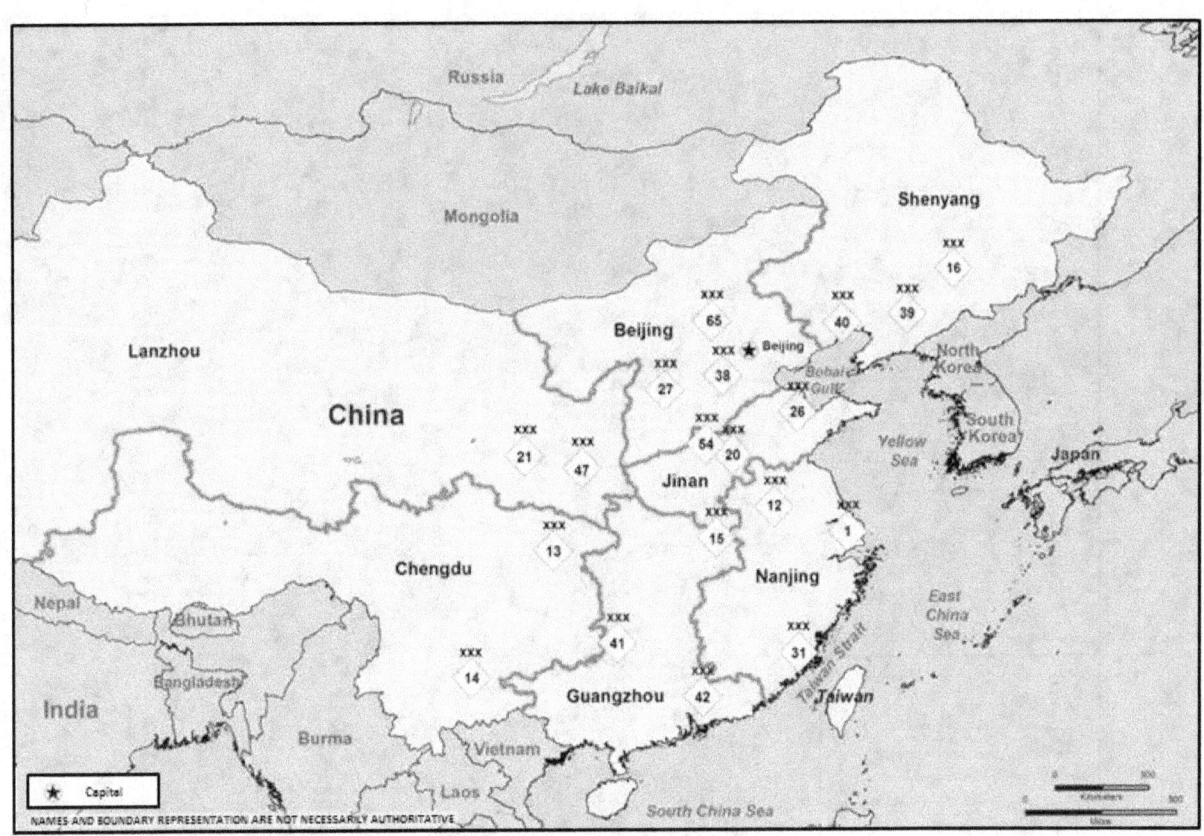

CHINA: Group Armies (GA) Primary Missions		
Shenyang MR	**Nanjing MR**	**Lanzhou MR**
16 GA – Defensive, Offensive CT	1 GA – Amphibious, Offensive CT	47 GA – Defensive, Offensive CT
39 GA – RRU, Offensive MF	12 GA – Amphibious, Offensive CT	21 GA – Offensive MF, Defensive
40 GA – Defensive, Offensive CT	31 GA – Amphibious, Offensive CT	
Beijing MR	**Guangzhou MR**	
65 GA – Defensive	15 Airborne – RRU, Offensive MF	
38 GA – RRU, Offensive MF	41 GA – Offensive CT, Amphibious	MR – Military Region
27 GA – Defensive	42 GA – Amphibious	MF – Mobile Force
Jinan MR	**Chengdu MR**	RRU – Rapid Reaction Unit
26 GA – Offensive CT, Defensive	13 GA – Defensive, Offensive CT	CT – Complex Terrain (mountain,
20 GA – Offensive CT, Defensive	14 GA – Defensive, Offensive CT	urban, jungle, etc.)
54 GA – Offensive MF, Amphibious		

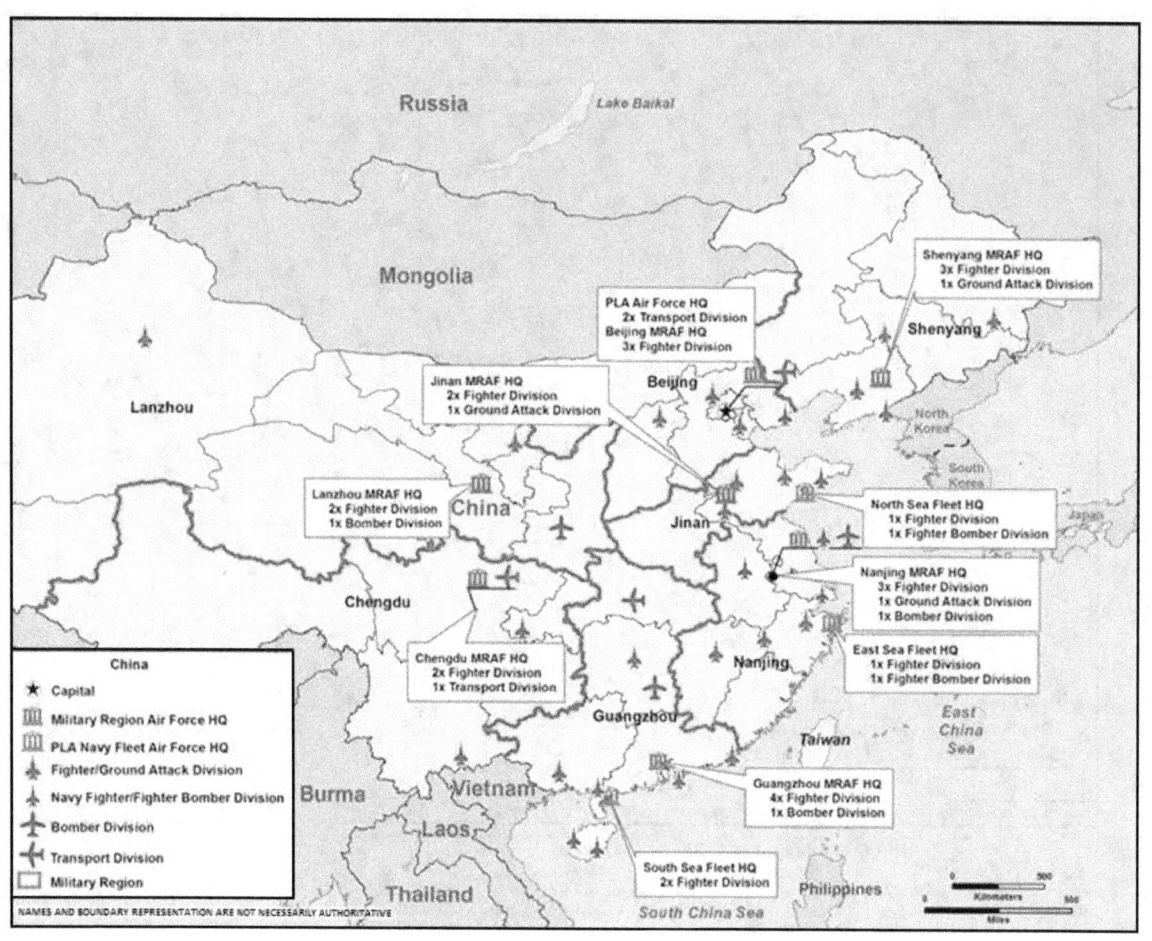

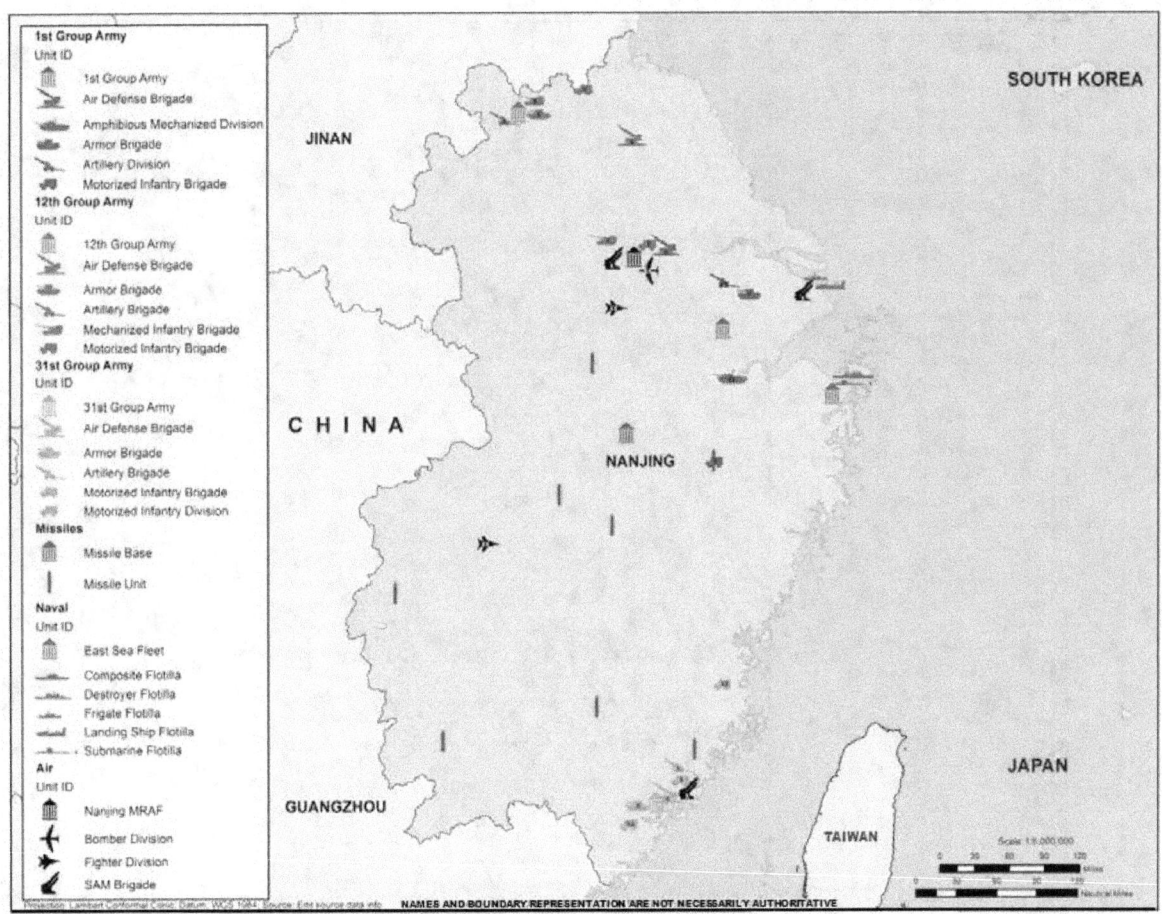

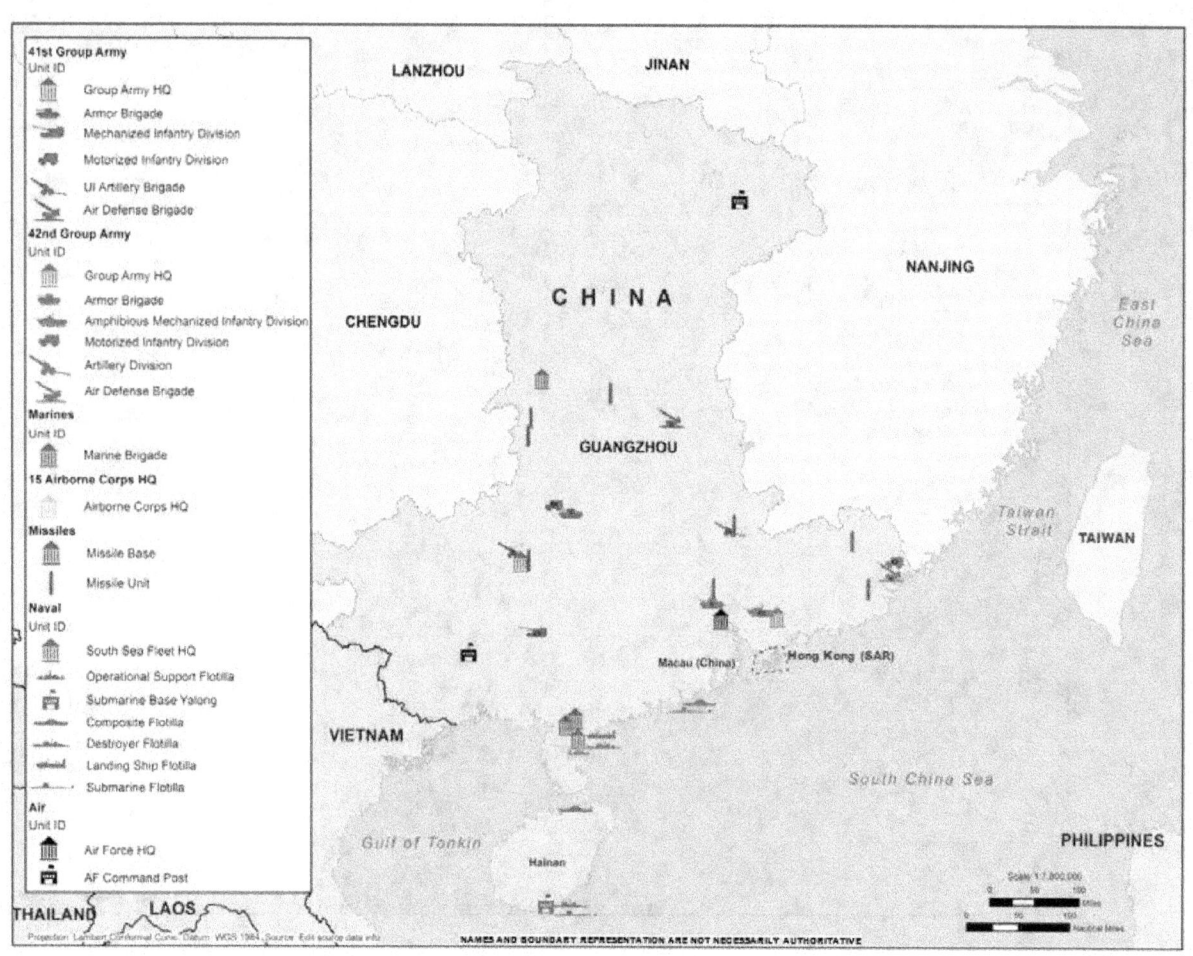

41st Group Army
Unit ID
- Group Army HQ
- Armor Brigade
- Mechanized Infantry Division
- Motorized Infantry Division
- UI Artillery Brigade
- Air Defense Brigade

42nd Group Army
Unit ID
- Group Army HQ
- Armor Brigade
- Amphibious Mechanized Infantry Division
- Motorized Infantry Division
- Artillery Division
- Air Defense Brigade

Marines
Unit ID
- Marine Brigade

15 Airborne Corps HQ
- Airborne Corps HQ

Missiles
- Missile Base
- Missile Unit

Naval
Unit ID
- South Sea Fleet HQ
- Operational Support Flotilla
- Submarine Base Yalong
- Composite Flotilla
- Destroyer Flotilla
- Landing Ship Flotilla
- Submarine Flotilla

Air
Unit ID
- Air Force HQ
- AF Command Post

LANZHOU

JINAN

NANJING

C H I N A

CHENGDU

East China Sea

GUANGZHOU

Taiwan Strait

TAIWAN

Macau (China)   Hong Kong (SAR)

VIETNAM

South China Sea

Gulf of Tonkin

Hainan

PHILIPPINES

Scale 1:7,800,000

THAILAND   LAOS

APPENDIX III: ADDITIONAL MAPS AND CHARTS

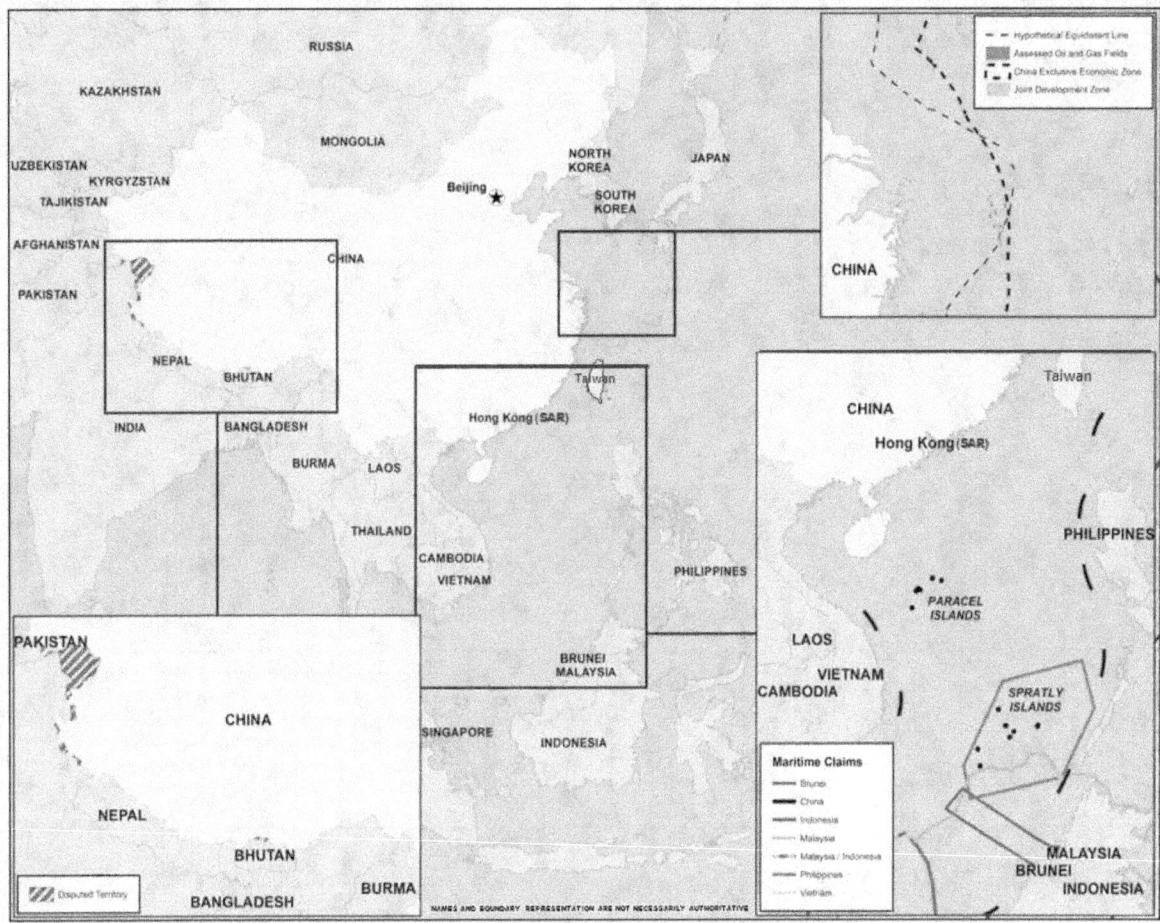

Figure 1: China's Sovereignty Claims.

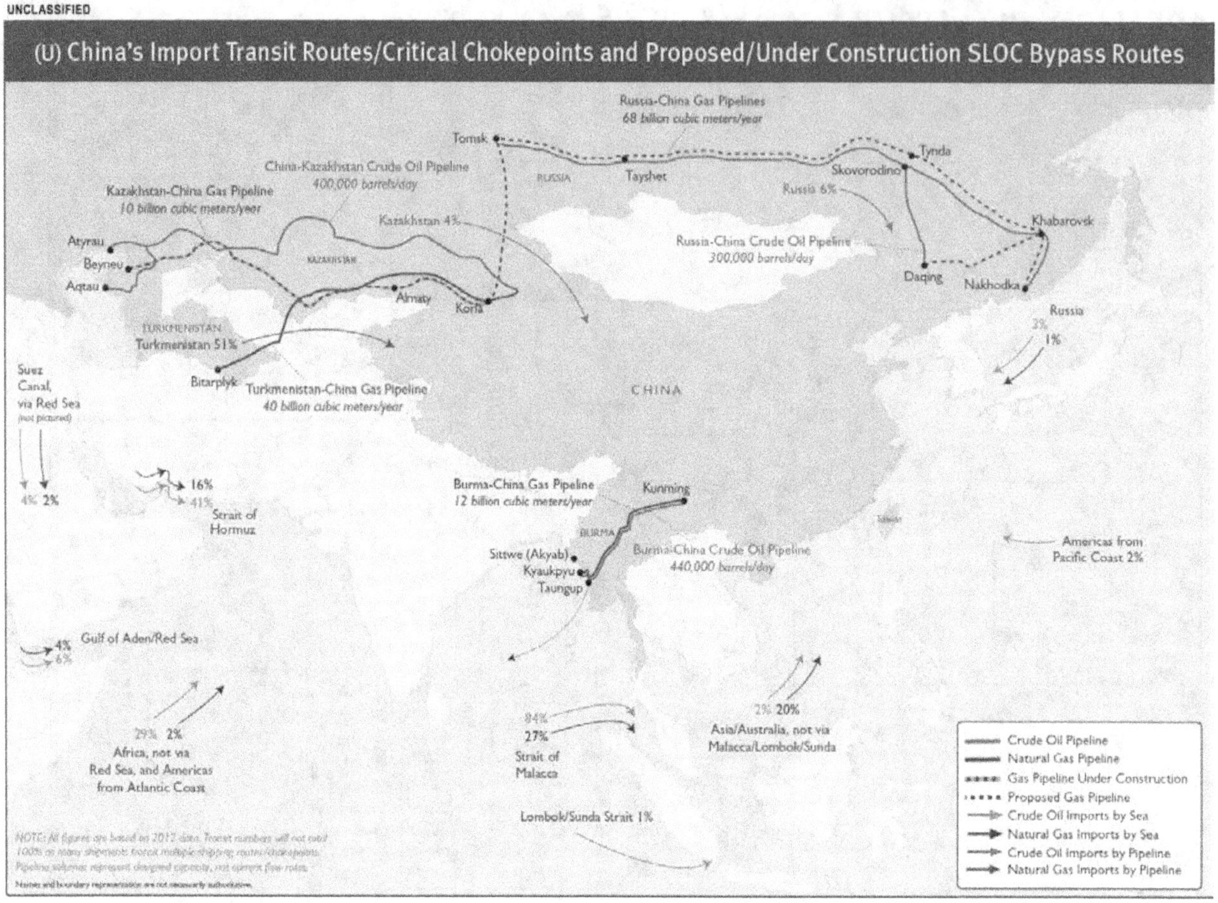

(U) China's Import Transit Routes/Critical Chokepoints and Proposed/Under Construction SLOC Bypass Routes

Figure 2: China's Import Transit Routes.

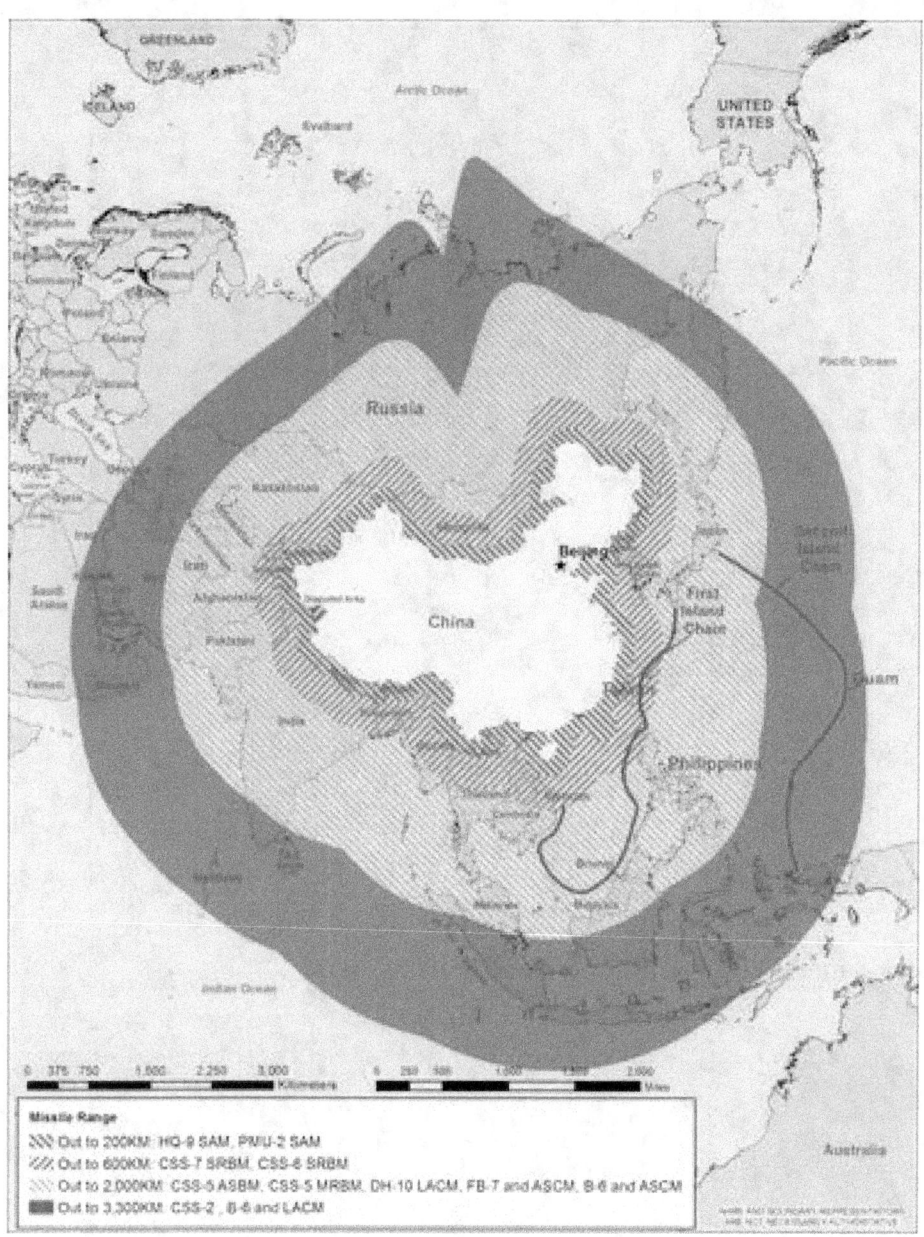

Figure 3: Conventional Strike Capabilities.

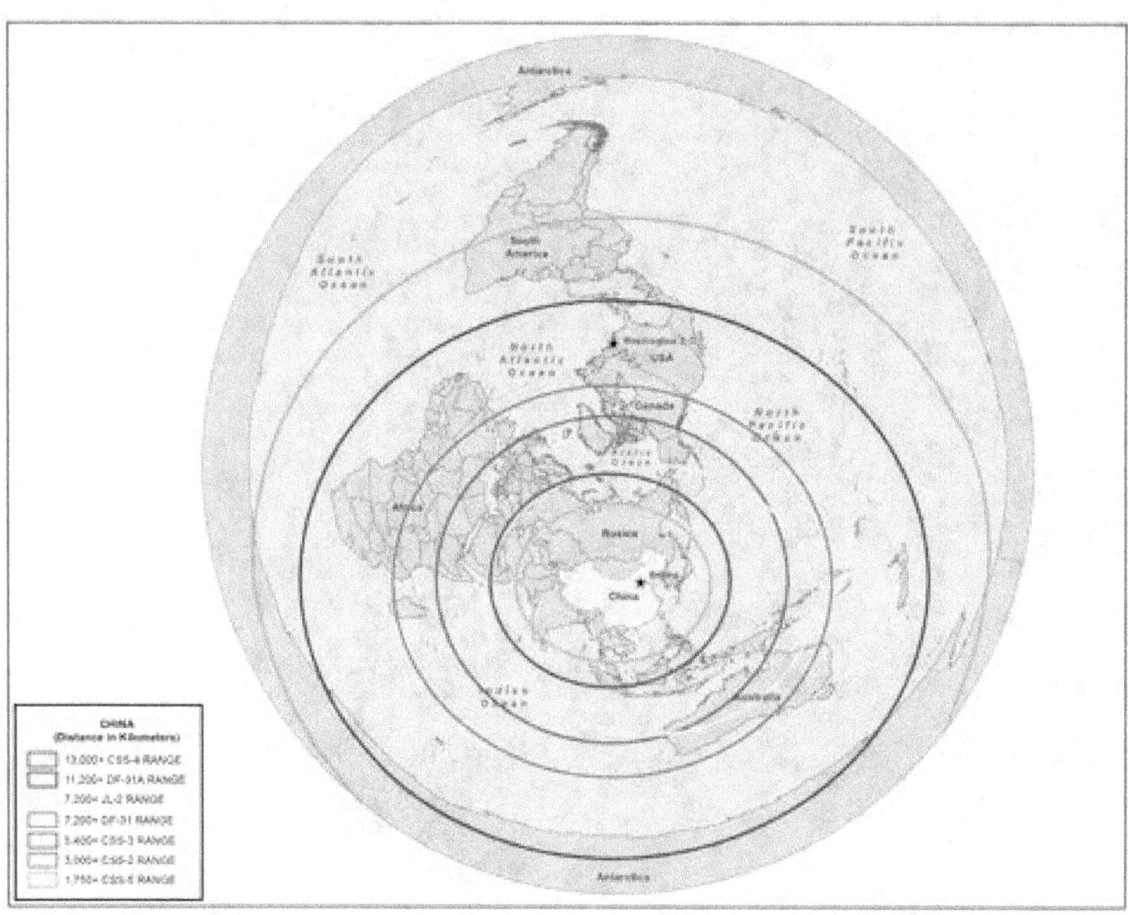

Figure 4: Medium and Intercontinental Range Ballistic Missiles.

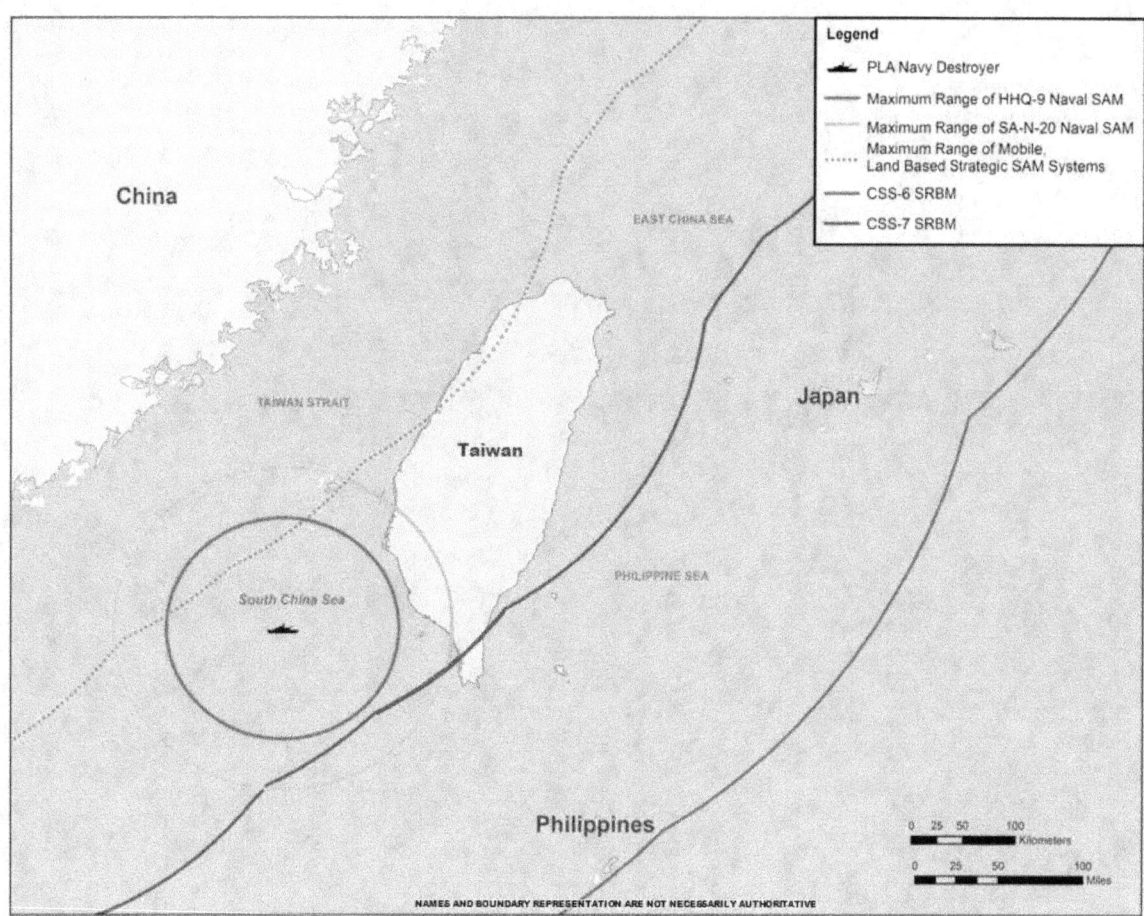

Figure 5: Taiwan Strait SAM and SRBM Coverage.